D0713679

Medium-Low Voice Edition

Foundations in Singing

A Basic Textbook in Vocal Technique and Song Interpretation

Fifth Edition

Medium-Low Voice Edition

Foundations in Singing

A Basic Textbook in Vocal Technique and Song Interpretation

Fifth Edition

Van A. Christy
Professor of Music Emeritus
University of California, Santa Barbara

as revised by
John Glenn Paton
Professor of Voice Emeritus
University of Colorado, Boulder

Book Team

Editor *Meredith M. Morgan*
Developmental Editor *Dean Robbins*
Production Coordinator *Carla D. Arnold*
Permissions Editor *Karen L. Storlie*

WCB **Wm. C. Brown Publishers**

President *G. Franklin Lewis*
Vice President, Publisher *Thomas E. Doran*
Vice President, Operations and Production *Beverly Kolz*
National Sales Manager *Virginia S. Moffat*
Advertising Manager *Ann M. Knepper*
Marketing Manager *Kathleen Nietzke*
Production Editorial Manager *Julie A. Kennedy*
Publishing Services Manager *Karen J. Slaght*
Manager of Visuals and Design *Faye M. Schilling*

Cover design by C. J. Petlick, Hunter Graphics

Consulting Editor Frederick Westphal

Contents

Song Contents

Musical theater songs

Popular songs and songs from motion pictures

Preface

After four editions and more than twenty years of successful use across the United States and Canada, the Wm. C. Brown Company Publishers undertook a complete revision of *Foundations in Singing* with the blessing of the original author, Dr. Van A. Christy. The fifth, revised edition follows the others in combining a textbook and a song anthology in one volume. It reflects changes in musical taste and the progress of research in vocal science, and it is published in two keys, medium high and medium low.

Dr. Christy's book has always served the needs of voice students in their first year of study, whether in high school or college, whether in private lessons or in group or class instruction. More and more teachers and institutions see the advantages of group instruction, especially at the beginning level, and the usefulness of a textbook to augment what students can learn during their limited instruction time. The fifth edition focuses on the essential needs of beginning students and uses positive, encouraging language throughout. The text reinforces the teacher's role, recognizing that the student-teacher relationship remains a vital factor in successful learning.

Ten chapters of this edition present a step-by-step approach to vocal technique that has been validated by years of experience: attitude, posture, breathing, tone and resonance, song preparation, English diction, performance, and extending the voice. Two new chapters, vocal physiology and music fundamentals, may be introduced at various times or assigned for outside reading, according to students' needs.

Inclusion of songs from Broadway and the world of popular music reflects their increasing acceptance over the last generation of voice teaching. Even voice teachers who limit their own singing to classical models have to recognize that not all popular singing is vocally abusive; the long careers of such fine performers as Mary Martin (*South Pacific* and *The Sound of Music*) and Barbara Cook (*The Music Man* and *Candide*) had to be based on healthful vocal usage. Furthermore, musicals such as *Cats* and *Phantom of the Opera* use vocal ranges that are just as wide as those used in operas. While opera and concert singing remain ideals for many of us, and while excellent classical music can be introduced early in musical study, our students deserve the help of a capable teacher in doing whatever style of music appeals to them.

Eleven songs for group singing are included in this edition because teachers have found them useful for energizing a group of students, warming up their voices, and introducing musical and vocal fundamentals. The remaining song literature has been thoroughly reviewed to eliminate songs that are outdated, to correct accumulated misprints, and to remove unauthentic expression markings that obscure the composers' original intentions. Primary sources from the seventeenth to the twentieth centuries have been used when they could be found.

A new Appendix A provides interpretive background for the songs, so that students learn the habit of approaching music thoughtfully. Background knowledge both awakens students' interest and helps them relate their songs to the cultural and historical worlds being studied in other disciplines. The notes go beyond what students can normally research on their own, including interpretations of mood, unusual words in the poems, and musical sources.

This edition builds on the strength of Dr. Christy's presentation of English diction (Chapters 6–8) and presents the complete International Phonetic Alphabet (IPA) for English in Appendix B. Vocal exercises for all of the English vowels are suggested in the belief that these can help the teacher correct some of the poor speech habits that slow down students' vocal progress. The text frequently reminds students of their responsibility to communicate with their listeners in understandable words.

For students who already have a foreign language background and want to use it in their singing, this edition gives songs in Italian, French, Spanish, and German. Whenever acceptable singing translations could be found, they are included (I prefer to hear a well-sung translation over a poorly sung foreign text). Mexican songs are included in this edition because the language of our North American neighbor is the most widely taught foreign language in the United States. Teachers whose vocal training was based on Italian find that Spanish has similar vocal advantages. French is our second most frequently taught language and is current in parts of Canada, so French is included also with one folk song and one *mélodie*.

Every foreign text is translated literally at the foot of the music page where the text first appears; this translation follows normal English word order and could be extracted for use in program notes. Foreign texts are retranslated word-for-word (not following English word order) in Appendix C, where IPA transcriptions are also given. (Information about foreign languages is limited to whatever is necessary for the songs at hand; a complete foreign language diction course is inappropriate for the first year of vocal study.) Again, the goal is to give students all of the information needed to perform songs with complete understanding, rather than in a haze of partial knowledge.

Acknowledgments

The task of writing a book for beginning singers has called on resources and experience from my entire life. I am indebted to the teachers who helped me earn my academic degrees: Franklin Bens and Sonia Essin at the Cincinnati Conservatory of Music and Julius Huehn at the Eastman School of Music. (Essin and Huehn were both students of Anna Schoen-René, a protege of Pauline Viardot-Garcia, who had the longest singing career of any of the famous Garcia family.) Other voice teachers whose words have entered this book include Laura May Titus of Cincinnati, R. Berton Coffin of Boulder, Oren Brown of New York City, and Mario Carta of Los Angeles. My musical life was strongly shaped by Parvin Titus and Melba Smith, my keyboard teachers, and by Hermann Reutter of Stuttgart, Germany, my mentor in *lieder*.

During seven years of teaching at the University of Wisconsin at Madison and sixteen years at the University of Colorado at Boulder, my students have taught me what worked and what didn't work in vocal pedagogy, and I am grateful for what I learned and for their patience with me. Since 1986 I have taught voice to acting students at the American Academy of Dramatic Arts-West in Pasadena, developing new techniques for teaching non-music-major students in groups of fifteen or more at a time. I am indebted to Jon Peck of the AADA-West, to all my voice faculty colleagues, and to the National Association of Teachers of Singing, to which we are all indebted for having fostered the sharing of professional knowledge to a degree that was unimaginable a generation ago.

The source notes in Appendix A refer to various libraries where I have worked; thanks go to their staff members and the benefactors and governments that support them. I have received helpful and specific comments from Dr. Julie Fortney and assistance with Mexican songs from Malena Boratgis and Professor Lucila Montoya Waldman.

Finally, my thanks and love go to my wife, Joan Thompson, who has supported this project in every possible way and who made this a better book by her keen ear for rhythm and nuance in language.

With the publication of *Foundations in Singing*, plans for its next revised edition will begin immediately. Readers and users of the book are sincerely invited to send comments and suggestions to me in care of the publisher, so that the next edition can be made even better.

John Glenn Paton
Los Angeles, California
(Emeritus Professor of Voice,
University of Colorado)

1 Freedom to Sing

Guiding questions: *Is singing worthwhile? Can I learn to sing with pleasure and success? How? Do I have either mental or physical blocks that will keep me from doing my best?*

WOULD you like to know how to sing well? Of course you would; almost everyone on earth would answer "Yes" to that question. Singing is such a natural part of human life that anthropologists find singing in all cultures, no matter how primitive they seem. Singing lulls babies to sleep, helps children learn language and physical coordination, carries messages of love that are deeper than simple words can say, energizes people to work together, consoles the bereaved, and does innumerable other good things for us, individually and as a society. As a result, the satisfaction of singing well is great, and so are the rewards that society gives to some who have an extraordinary gift for singing.

Can I learn to sing?

Again, the answer is "Yes." Any person who has a normal speaking voice and can "carry a tune" (or can learn to do so) can learn to sing well and to derive enjoyment from singing. In other words, you have a musical instrument in your possession, and it is awaiting only liberation and knowledge of how to use it.

If you have difficulty believing this, you are not alone. Many people approach singing with fear, often because others have told them that they "can't sing." Let's look at the reasons why "fear of singing" affects some of us.

Many children live in homes where no one sings with them; they have no chance to learn the natural, but complex coordination between hearing a musical tone and producing it with their voices. Many children have no music teacher in school, and classroom teachers may lack the time or the skill to lead group singing or to help those who have a hard time joining in.

Some children, both boys and girls, enjoy singing in the early grades but stop singing when they enter puberty because they feel insecure with the new physical sensations that go along with having an adult larynx. At this time in life a young person is especially vulnerable to criticism and to being put down by others.

Is it any wonder that many people become non-singing adults? They admire good singers, but they expect the worst if they were ever to try singing. The idea of singing a song in front of other people is embarrassing, even threatening, to them. They stay silent, or perhaps they sing along with the radio when they are alone. They do not know that with a bit of courage and a short course of instruction they can start to have fun singing with others and for others.

The easy availability of music on recordings and radio can even add to our "fear of singing." Unrealistically, we compare ourselves with professional singers in studio recordings, and we become overly self-critical. That problem goes away when we find out how our listeners prefer a live performance to any music that comes through an amplifier.

Recordings and radio are convenient, but they cannot replace our own self-expression. If we lived without electricity and batteries, we would often sing to fill up the emptiness of a lonely place or to keep up our spirits while we work. Think of singing with a group of friends around a campfire and what fun that is!

If you came through childhood and adolescence with confidence and a positive attitude about singing, count yourself lucky. You have a basis of confidence from which you can begin immediately to improve your singing and increase your knowledge about your voice. As you progress, remember to encourage others along the way; never cut down anyone who sincerely tries to sing well.

Most people think of singing as an inborn talent. You will find that singing is a skill that can be learned from a capable teacher, improved with practice and experience, and reinforced by positive experiences with others. Yes, talent plays a major role, but you will find that with instruction and practice your voice will improve in ways that you cannot foresee now.

How will I improve my singing?

Learning to sing is both a mental and a physical process, one that includes both intellectual learning and the training of muscular habits. Essentially, you will start with the vocal capabilities you now have, including both speaking and singing. With increased awareness of how your voice works, you will use daily practice to form good vocal habits and to eliminate any vocal habits that are causing trouble. You will extend your abilities by setting step-by-step goals that allow you to experience success and to feel growing confidence.

With a positive, enthusiastic approach toward learning to sing, you yourself are the most important factor in the learning process. The second most important factor is your teacher, a person who cares about helping you to sing better and has the skill and experience to do so. If you want to know about your teacher's training and musical career, it's OK to ask. You can make your teacher's work much easier by participating actively in the learning process, which includes regular class attendance, daily practice outside of class, asking and responding to questions in class.

It is natural to feel hesitant about trying new skills in any area, and even more so in an activity as emotional as singing. You can help the learning process greatly if you recognize such normal feelings without indulging in displays of shy behavior, such as giggling, clowning, apologies, and excuses. Such self-centered actions only delay your real progress.

The most basic process in voice instruction is that your teacher will *listen to you sing and suggest how to sing better*. This process may start at the very first meeting, either with a song that you have prepared or with impromptu singing of a simple song like "Happy Birthday" or with an exercise that the teacher demonstrates before asking you to sing it. After you have taken this first plunge, the teacher will introduce new concepts by demonstration and description with the help of readings in this book. All through your lessons, the teacher will listen for the best sounds that you can make, because it is important to notice what techniques work best for you and to use them more and more.

If you are taking private voice lessons, you have two main advantages: your teacher's full attention for the length of the lesson and the privilege of moving ahead at your own pace.

If you are receiving instruction in a small group or in a voice class, you have other advantages:

- you will gain confidence from seeing that other people have fears and difficulties that are much like your own;
- you can try out new techniques in the safety of group vocalizing;
- you will trust your teacher more after seeing how other students improve with guidance;
- you will understand new concepts better through questions and discussions with your peers;
- you will lose your qualms about singing in front of others, especially as class members give and receive mutual encouragement.

You have some responsibilities. If you are going to miss a private lesson, the teacher needs to know at least a day ahead in order to give your lesson time to someone else. If you arrive late or miss a lesson without advance notice, it is time lost and you cannot expect the teacher to make it up.

If you are in a voice class, remember that you are a participating individual, not just a seat number in a lecture hall. If you arrive late or leave early, you disrupt the work that others are doing. If you miss too many classes, the process goes on for others without you. You cannot "cram" the experience of vocal growth by extra practicing before an exam.

Between meetings with your teacher, practice daily, read your assignments, and learn the assigned music. You may also be expected to learn more about singing through assigned listening and through attending musical performances.

For your practicing you will need a solitary, quiet place, where you can make vocal experiments without worrying about who hears you or what anyone thinks. A living room with family members around is not the right place, nor is a thin-walled apartment with sleeping neighbors. A practice room in a music school is ideal, or you might be able to rent a space at a local church. You need some means of producing specific pitches, at best a piano or a synthesizer, at least a pitch pipe or an audiocassette tape with the recorded pitches you need. A large mirror is also very useful for reasons that you will learn later.

If you have heard a recording of your own speaking voice, you know already that we do not sound to ourselves the way we sound to others. For this reason an audiocassette player is an essential piece of equipment. A small cassette recorder does not reproduce your voice quality perfectly, but even a poor recording is absolutely honest about whether you sing on time and in tune.

Take your cassette recorder to every class and, with your teacher's permission, use it often. The first few times you sing or vocalize in class you may be too nervous or excited to get a clear idea of how well you performed. Your recorder will let you hear again what comments were made and whether or not your singing actually improved as a result.

Physical freedom

Singing feels good; and we feel good as a result of singing, provided that our bodies are healthy and we use them correctly. Unfortunately, most of us have ways of using our bodies that interfere with comfort. The next chapter will discuss breathing and posture in greater detail, but at the very start we need ways of assuring that our bodies are free for singing.

Physical freedom to sing means that the muscles we need for the activity of singing are ready to work without interference from other muscles. In order to understand why interference occurs, we need to think about the way muscles work.

Muscle tissue characteristically has the ability to contract. When we use a muscle, it receives a message through the nervous system and contracts. When we finish using that muscle, it should relax, but it may not relax completely. Some muscle fibers may remain tense, leaving the muscle partially contracted. If you drive on a busy freeway or if you carry heavy books from class to class, this kind of residual tension might give you sore shoulders or back pain. You will feel better about singing if you get rid of such tensions first.

When a muscle is activated, there may be partial activation of a neighboring muscle also, because connections exist between neighboring nerves. This is a second cause of unnecessary tension. Many of us have slight tensions in our speaking habits, for instance, because the tiny muscles involved are so close to each other.

A third source of unnecessary tension is that, during rest, the nervous system continues to send out occasional signals to the muscles, constantly testing to be sure that the pathways for nerve impulses are open. These signals cause slight contractions of the muscles, and this is a reason why our long muscles grow shorter during sleep and feel stiff when we awaken.

Stretching

One of the best ways to dispel tension is through *stretching* the concerned muscle groups. Gentle, patient stretching provides time for the muscle fibers to give up tight holds that they no longer need. When a stretch is released, the muscle fibers return to a neutral, relaxed position. Massage is another way of allowing muscles to give up unwanted tension.

Try the following exercises for a few minutes at a time and, with the help of your teacher, choose the ones that help you most. Three pieces of advice go with every exercise.

- If any exercise causes pain, stop it immediately.
- Breathe in and out normally, without holding your breath.
- A stretched muscle is in a weak position; do not shock it by a bouncing movement.

Exercises

1.1 *Rib Stretch.* Standing with your weight on the left foot, reach up with your right arm and stretch toward the ceiling. Increase the stretch in your torso by bending your right knee. While continuing to stretch, move your arm forward and back slowly, 10–15 seconds. Relax, then repeat on the other side. Purpose: to stretch the small muscles between your ribs, the intercostals, so that you can use full lung capacity when you want to.

1.2 *Sleepyhead.* Let your head drop forward toward your chest without collapsing your shoulders, and then let it fall to one side about 45 degrees. Lift your head, then let it fall forward again and to the other side about 45 degrees. Stay with each position for a few seconds. Let your head fall into position by its own weight, rather than placing. Purpose: to stretch the strong muscles that hold the head erect.

(Caution: you may like to loosen your neck by rotating your head in a large circle, but that is not entirely safe for everyone. *Sleepyhead* is relatively safe. Again, if any exercise causes pain, stop it immediately.)

1.3 *Rag Doll.* Let your head drop forward, but then roll the shoulders forward and gently bend your back a little at a time, from the top down, until you have bent forward as far as you can without bending the knees. *Do not bounce* in this position, but just enjoy the stretch in your lower back. Let your head and arms hang loosely. Flex (bend) your knees a few times to increase the stretch gently. Straighten up slowly and gently. Purpose: to release back and neck tensions that may interfere with good posture and breathing.

1.4 *Neck Stretchers.* Reach over your head with your right arm until your fingers are just above your left ear. Let the weight of your arm pull your head to the right so that you feel a stretch in your left shoulder. Stay with the stretch for 15–20 seconds, then feel how your head "floats" up to normal position. Repeat the stretch on the other side. Variations: use your right arm (reaching over your head from front to back) to pull your head straight forward; use your arms to draw your head down to left and to right at 45 degree angles. Stay with each stretch for 15–20 seconds. Purpose: to release neck and shoulder tensions, often relieving tension pains in the upper back.

1.5 *Neck Massage.* With the flat fingers of your right hand massage the left side of your neck, then change sides. Enjoy the feeling. Purpose: to release tension and improve circulation in the front of the neck.

1.6 *Yawn.* Really yawn. Silently. If you don't know how to yawn at will, fake it at first and then learn to yawn at home in front of a mirror. Purpose: to stretch the back of the mouth open by lifting the soft palate and lowering the back of the tongue.

To understand the importance of yawning, swallow first. Feel the tension in your throat as the tongue rises and the soft palate closes downward against it. The swallowing muscles are very strong because we use them frequently, awake or asleep. Yawning stretches and frees them. Other teachers may be insulted if you yawn in class, but your voice teacher likes it!

1.7 *Hum Slide.* Imagine a note a little higher than the pitch where you usually speak. Hum that note and let your voice slide downward. When you have done this several times comfortably, think a little higher pitch and slide down from that one. It is not important exactly what pitches you sing. Purpose: to explore the pitch range that you can use with comfort from the beginning. Work moderately high without trying for an extreme.

1.8 *Hum Slide 5th.* To musicians, a 5th is the distance between the first and fifth notes of a scale. You can easily imagine a 5th by mentally singing the opening of "The Star-Spangled Banner": the distance between the first and third notes is the interval of a 5th. As in "hum slide," hum any pitch and slide down to another pitch a 5th lower. You may think "Oh, say!" while you hum in order to get the interval right. Slide down-up-down-up-down, starting on the upper note and ending on the lower one. Again, what particular pitch you sing is not important; keep changing, higher and lower. Purpose: exploring your comfortable singing range with more control of pitch.

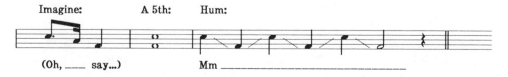

1.9 *Who Slide 5th.* Sing the syllable "Who" softly, using the same pattern as in "hum slide 5th." Phonetically, the syllable "who" begins with the consonant *h*, which assures that the breath is moving freely and gently before the singing tone is heard. Purpose: exploring your comfortable range with a quiet singing tone.

Additional reading

A stimulating, fun book about mental attitudes and about solving problems in music and life is:
A Soprano on Her Head by Eloise Ristad. Real People Press, Moab, Utah, 1982.

For safe ways to improve your physical fitness:
Stretching by Bob Anderson. Shelter Publications (Random House), 1980.

2 Breath and the Body

Guiding questions: *How should I sit or stand to sing? How do singers breathe?*

SAY the word "posture" to a group of people, and a number of them will stiffen up. They may even have learned in school to imitate soldiers at attention.

Good posture involves more than just erectness, and certainly not stiffness. Posture includes both readiness for action and the way the body is used during the action. If the body is held stiffly, then any action we want to take must work against that stiffness; if it is held off-balance, then we have to overcome that before the right action can take place.

Singing posture

Good posture for singing means using the body in a balanced way that lets our breathing muscles work easily and lets the sound that we imagine be produced without any physical interference.

It is true that accomplished performers can sing in almost any position, even lying down or standing on their heads. Performers in musical theater must be able to sing while dancing, and in India and many other countries singers sit down to perform. But while we are discovering and freeing our voices, we want the best possible conditions. An erect posture gives us the freedom we want for singing.

Unfortunately, what feels like natural posture for the beginning student is often a faulty posture that must first be corrected before proper breath control can be established.

Here are some characteristics of good singing posture:

Figure 2.1

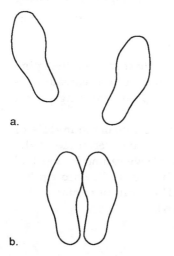

a.

b.

1. Feet: Place your heels a few inches apart with your toes turned out slightly. One foot may be slightly forward of your center of gravity, the other slightly back. Balance your weight evenly, and keep both feet on the floor. The position in Figure 2.1a gives you a firm basis, but allows you to move in any direction with a minimum of effort.

   Avoid: standing with the feet too close together, as in Figure 2.1b, so that your body either stands stiffly or weaves around like a palm tree; lifting your heels off the floor for high notes, which betrays mental anxiety; placing your weight on one leg so that the torso is twisted and the breath muscles work asymmetrically.

2. Legs: Straight, but not locked rigidly at the knees.

3. Torso: Level, both at hip height and at shoulder height. The abdominal muscles in the front and the spinal column in the back work together to support and straighten the torso. With the help of active back muscles, the ribs are able to expand to their widest position at will.

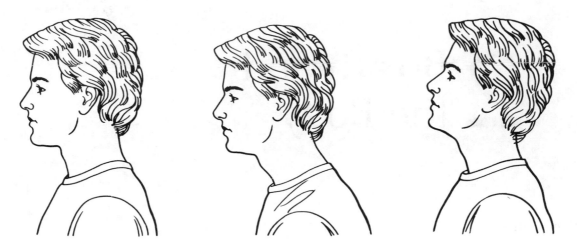

Figure 2.2

Avoid curving your back too far inward. A swaybacked position weakens the spine and makes it prone to injury. Because this posture throws the viscera (the "innards") too far forward, the abdominal muscles are stretched into a weakened state and cannot give us the flexible breath control we need.

4. Shoulders: Level. Let them relax downward and backward.

    Some of us hunch up our shoulders because of fear of insecurity, for instance, before a difficult note. This fear reflex makes our listeners uncomfortable, too. Relaxing our shoulders counteracts the reflex and helps our sense of confidence.

    Also, if we let our shoulders slouch forward, wanting to look casual and easygoing, we may just look lazy or uninterested or nonconfident. Slouching throws the neck and head out of line, causing some problems described later on.

5. Neck and Head: Let them rise effortlessly toward the ceiling, as if a puppeteer were lifting you from above. Imagine a hook set into your head, directly over and between your ears, and a cord pulling up on the hook. Let your head remain level so that your eyes look straight ahead, neither down nor up.

    Avoid stretching your neck forward, so that your head is forward of your center of gravity (Figure 2.2b), and tilting your head up (Figure 2.2c). These common faults cause many problems. For this reason, head alignment deserves a whole section to itself.

Head alignment

Knowing that a person's spine runs up the back, it is easy to think that the spine connects to the back of the head. If this were true, the weight of the head (usually more than 11 pounds) would be held in front of the spine, requiring a great deal of muscular energy to hold it up.

In fact, the spine curves sharply inward to a position near the middle of the neck. (Just below this curve we can easily feel the upper vertebrae of the back; but the curve carries the spine into the neck, where we can no longer feel individual vertebrae). The top vertebra slants forward, and its forward tip has two small surfaces on which the skull is supported. The point of contact is between our ears, close behind the back wall of the throat.

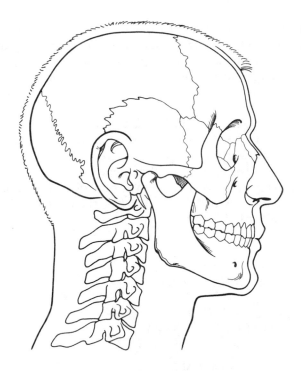

When the head is correctly balanced on the spine, directly over the body's center of gravity, it takes little or no muscular effort to keep it aligned. To understand this, try turning a cereal bowl upside down and balancing it on the eraser end of a pencil.

Clearly, if the spine slumps forward and the weight of the head is constantly in front of the body's center of gravity, the muscles in the back of the neck have to support the head and keep it from falling. As pointed out in chapter 1, tension can spread from those muscles to the front of the neck and interfere with singing.

Another problem with a slouched posture is that it more or less stretches the muscles at the front of the neck. If the neck muscles are stretched, their freedom of response is limited.

Avoid stretching your neck to reach for high notes. Children do so because their soft voice boxes need the pull of external muscles, but adults do not need to stretch their necks.

With the body correctly positioned and the head comfortably balanced on the spinal column, we are ready to learn how singers breathe.

Learn to breathe

We have been breathing at an average of twenty times per minute all our lives, breathing faster when we exercise and using our breath to speak and shout all we want. Even so, singing makes special demands on our breath.

1. The length of the musical phrases we can sing depends both on the volume of air in our lungs and on our ability to release air slowly and steadily.

2. Our ability to sing louder and softer and to sing with expression and variety depends directly on our ability to vary the rate of airflow.

3. Musical rhythm often requires us to take air in quickly between phrases.

We must be able to release breath energy at a precisely controlled rate for a desired length of time and to renew the energy quickly. This sums up what people commonly call "breath control." If "control" has a negative meaning for you, you can use a more positive phrase: "breath management."

To achieve efficient breath management, we use the parts of the body that combine flexibility and muscular strength, especially the area of the lower ribs and the abdominal wall. Although many muscle groups are involved, we do not need to analyze all of them. The next section attempts to describe the process as simply as possible.

The breathing mechanism

Air fills the lungs, two spongy sacks that are passive, not muscular. The lungs are contained in the bony cage of the ribs, and if the rib cage expands, air rushes into them automatically.

The rib cage, as a whole, has some flexibility. Individual ribs, being bone, do not stretch or bend. They move somewhat like curved bucket handles, fanning out wider when they are lifted by the chest and back muscles. All ribs are attached in the back to the spine.

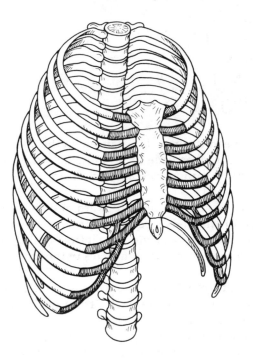

The uppermost ribs are attached to the breastbone (sternum) in front and to the spine behind; they have little of the mobility we need for singing. A well-trained singer does not move these ribs very much because they are already high in correct posture and to use them further involves unwanted action of neck muscles.

The middle ribs, five, six, and seven, move more freely because they are attached to the sternum in front by flexible cartilage. The next three ribs move even more freely because each is attached to the next rib above by cartilage. All of these lower ribs can be lifted and moved outward to increase the space in the lungs and let air in. They can also be lowered and narrowed to push air out. This is a useful way of releasing breath energy, but because it involves moving rigid and rather heavy bones it may not give us as much ease and precision of movement as we desire.

The most flexible part of the rib cage is its floor, formed by a complex muscle called the diaphragm. The name *diaphragm* comes from Greek roots that mean "to enclose completely," and the diaphragm closes the bottom of the breath

Figure 2.3

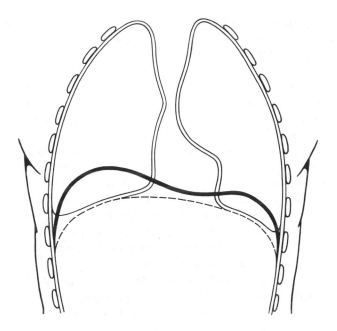

chamber, the thorax, separating it from the digestive organs below. The diaphragm is attached at its edges to the spine, the sternum, and the lowest ribs. It has openings for the "food pipe" (esophagus) and blood vessels to pass through it to the lower body.

In a relaxed state, the diaphragm has the shape of two domes, one under each lung. When the diaphragm contracts, its domelike curves flatten downward, creating more space in the chest cavity and allowing air to rush in (see the dotted line in Figure 2.3). This action pushes down on viscera below, causing them to push the abdominal wall outward.

Sometimes people speak of "breathing from the diaphragm" and pat their tummies. They are really talking about the upper part of the abdominal wall, the epigastrium, which moves outward when the diaphragm lowers. The diaphragm itself is inside the body, where it is neither seen nor felt.

If the movements of these muscles become confusing, remember a simple point: When we breathe in, the body becomes larger; when we breathe out or sing, it becomes smaller.

As we sing, the muscles at the front and sides of the epigastrium and/or the ribs (the "costal" area) must move in. It is up to us to decide what part of the musculature will move in and how quickly. "Costal-epigastrium breathing" describes a balanced use of these muscles.

If the costal and epigastrium muscles work together and nothing slows them down, they empty the lungs very quickly, much too quickly for singing. We slow down the process and control the airflow by using opposing muscles, or antagonists. We deliberately keep the ribs expanded for as long as possible, and we let the diaphragm continue the downward push that brought the air in. This happens simply as a result of our decision to breathe out slowly, even though we cannot control the diaphragm consciously. (The diaphragm has no proprioceptors, no nerves that report sensations of pain or position to the brain.)

In order to understand the opposition (antagonism) of the breathing muscles, put one hand on top of the other with the palms together and push them against each other. One hand pushes down like the diaphragm, while the other moves up like the upward and inward pull of the abdominal wall. The result is a slow movement that can be precisely controlled.

When we have this slow, steady movement combined with a well-produced tone, we say that we have "breath support" or that the tone is well "supported."

Theories of breath support

All singers use the process described above, but individual singers and voice teachers explain the process in different ways and emphasize different parts of it in their practicing and singing. The result is that one can hear and read many theories about breath support.

Some singers stress sensations of downward and outward pushing, while others think in terms of more relaxed, flowing movements. Some singers concentrate on the epigastrium area, while others use the whole abdominal muscle wall as a single unit. Others say that the "secret" of support lies in the back muscles, which certainly help out by preventing the fall of the ribs. Still others believe that the whole process will occur automatically if our mental concepts of tone are correct. Regarding such a complex musculature, it is no wonder that artists use it in a variety of ways.

In action, breath support means keeping the tone flowing evenly, freely, and firmly. We may find that at times we need to concentrate on holding the breath back, while at other times we need to remind ourselves not to block the outward flow.

It is well to emphasize that breath control also involves tone control and is dependent for success on efficient resonance. Breath management and good tone develop together; both must be mastered over an extended period.

Interaction between posture and breath action

You have a foundation for good breath action if:

1.   The spine feels flexibly stretched, lifted by the bouyancy of the head.
2.   The chest remains comfortably high and quiet during singing, not rigidly high, as when a soldier stands at attention.
3.   The ribs widen by action of the back muscles before inhalation starts. If this is not done, you will probably lift the chest to inhale, starting a motion that pumps the chest up on every inhalation and collapses it on every exhalation.

Phases of breath action

In daily life we think of breath in two phases, in and out. For singing we can consider four phases: inhalation, turnaround, exhalation, and recovery.

1.   *Inhalation* is taken through both the mouth and nose, or through the nose only if time allows. With the ribs already somewhat lifted and widened, you sense the throat as open and relaxed and the body as opening deeply when the diaphragm descends and the abdominals relax. Inhale positively and deeply, but don't "cram" the lungs with air. Imagine the coming note so that you will be ready with the right pitch and the right vowel or consonant. Let in enough air to sing the coming phrase, plus a little reserve.
2.   *Turnaround* is a split second when your diaphragm has reached its lowest point and the abdominals begin to resist it. Let your vocal cords remain open. Your vocal instrument is ready to sing.
3.   *Exhalation* produces the tone. Let a gentle movement of your abdominals, working slowly against the resistance of the diaphragm, slightly compress your air supply; it rises through the voice box, creating the tone.

Abdominal action alone is enough for a short phrase. A longer phrase may also require the ribs to move inward at the end. Only in emergencies do we fully collapse the rib cage because often this causes muscular tension and a poor sound.

4. *Recovery* is the opposite of the turnaround phase: a moment of relaxation for the working muscles. Let the abdomen relax outward (without losing your posture). If the ribs have moved, let them regain their wide position; otherwise, do nothing with them. If you have time for a rest, breathe normally; if the music goes on quickly, you must reverse the flow of air as quickly as you did in the turnaround phase. An experienced singer recovers rapidly for the next phrase; a beginner may "bog down" after singing a taxing phrase, unable to go on.

Some experts speak of all four phases as parts of one smoothly continuous cycle. You can visualize it as a circular movement or as the lapping of waves on the shore of the ocean.

Upside-down breathing

Toddlers breathe correctly, but by adulthood many of us have lost the knack. If you breathe by lifting your chest and pulling in your abdomen, as many people do, then you are not really getting a "deep breath" but a high, tense breath. You are "filling up" instead of "breathing deep."

Upside-down breathing causes at least three problems:

1. Your abdominal muscles are stiff before you start to sing, so they cannot help move the air out.

2. In breathing out, you have to lower and contract your rib cage, affecting your posture. The tension of the chest muscles also affects the neck muscles.

3. Because the weight of your ribs is providing some of the air compression, you have less resilience than if the lower muscles were doing the work.

You need to retrain your breathing reflexes, a process that may take several days or several weeks. Be sure to relax the abdominal muscles during inhalation so that they can start to work correctly during exhalation.

Bodybuilding

A weak or sick person cannot expect to sing well, and in chapter 11 you can learn more about keeping your voice healthy. Anyone who is below normal in physical vitality or weak in chest development will profit from practicing the exercises given here several times a day and should probably start a regular program of physical exercise.

Bodybuilding, however, is not our goal; a normal physique is strong enough for voice study. Some very muscular students find it hard to relax their neck and abdomen muscles enough to sing freely. Exercise to invigorate and strengthen your body, not to exhaust it.

Students sometimes wonder out loud whether breathing exercises will thicken their waistlines. Quite the opposite! Good abdominal muscles are essential to a good figure. Incidentally, they also support the back muscles and help us avoid back pains.

Exercises

Repeat the stretching exercises from chapter 1, keeping them as part of your daily warm-up. Try out the sensation of letting your head float toward the ceiling, with your spine dangling from your head and the shoulders and arms relaxed. Feel how pleasant this is, and remind yourself of it often. Add the next exercises.

2.1 *Shoulder Roll.* In a circular motion, let both shoulders move back, up, forward, and down. Make at least four continuous circles; reverse direction and make at least four more circles in the opposite direction. End the cycle by moving the shoulders back and then down. Purpose: to release any tensions that are stiffening the shoulder muscles.

Notice that you can do this exercise with the chest either lifted or collapsed. Naturally, a lifted position is better, but this exercise shows that the shoulders are independent from the chest position and do not hold the chest up. Always let your shoulders remain relaxed and low during singing.

2.2 *Abdominal Action.* Standing erect, raise both arms toward the ceiling, letting the rib cage rise as a result. Alternately tense and relax the abdominals. As they tense and move in, make the consonant sound "sh." As they relax and move outward, let air come into the lungs. Do this in a rhythm, alternating one second of sound with one second of silence. Purpose: to sense the bellowslike action of the abdominals and to overcome any stiffness in this area. Take turns with a partner and compare notes to be sure the abdomen is moving in the right direction.

2.3 *Rib-widening.* Place your fists against your sides, so that you feel the width of your rib cage. Exhale fully, so that your rib cage is as narrow as possible. Let your ribs relax and widen, and then consciously spread them as wide as possible. Your ribs should push your fists outward at least one inch on each side. Hold for about four seconds and then relax. Purpose: awareness of the potential expansion of the rib cage. Check your partner's rib expansion with your fists against her or his lower back at the sides, and then let yourself be checked the same way. You can learn a lot by comparison.

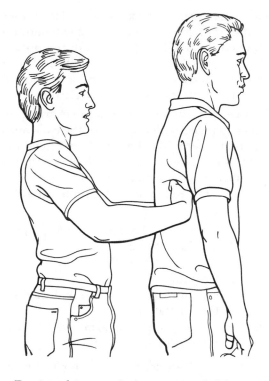

During this exercise you are probably using rib-breathing only. That's why this exercise is for discovery, not for daily drill. Repeat it only when you need a reminder of your vital capacity.

2.4 *Full Breath Action.* Phases 1 and 2. During a slow, deep inhalation through the nose, with the throat open, free, and relaxed, raise the arms steadily from the sides, palms down, on a slow count of 1–2–3–4, until they meet over the head. At this point the ribs have their maximum expansion, the diaphragm has lowered, and the abdominals have relaxed outward.

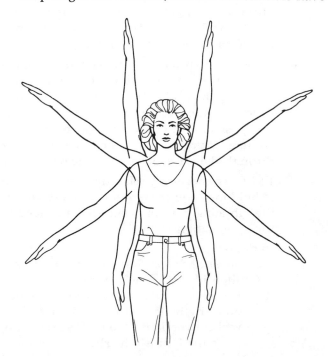

Full Breath Action. Phases 3 and 4. Hold the chest and ribs steady and high as the arms come down during exhalation on a hissing "sh" or "ss" to a slow count of 1–2–3–4. Maintain the outward, lifting rib expansion until the abdominals have finished their lift inward against the diaphragm. Purpose: to build a habit of sustaining an open rib cage and free, vital breathing with the muscles around the waistline.

Notice that when you repeat the exercise in a continuous rhythm, the ribs stay expanded with the help of the back muscles. Once lifted and expanded by the first arm lift, the ribs do not need to be lifted again; the arm movement simply reminds us of their position and helps us correct any temporary slump. Practice this daily until your back muscles can sustain a singing posture for several minutes at a time.

Variations:

a. Increase the exhalation count to 6 or 8. Keep the inhalation count at 4 or reduce it to 2.
b. Change the "ss" to "zz" or "vv," so that the vocal cords are used for the sound.
c. Open your mouth and speak the syllable "huh," letting it last as long as the inhalation.
d. Eventually, omit the arm action when you no longer need constant reminders of expansion.

Voice exercises

Repeat all of the exercises from chapter 1; they are part of your daily warm-up. Do them with awareness of the breath action you learned in this chapter.

2.5 *Panting.* Place the fingertips on the stomach wall in the epigastrium area just below the breastbone. With the chest comfortably high, quickly inhale a vigorous breath (the fingertips move outward). Release the breath suddenly, speaking a "huh" sound. Repeat vigorously and rhythmically in a series of panting pulsations. Use an enthusiastic speaking level, pitched a little bit higher than your normal, relaxed speech. Encourage a strong "kickback" feeling under your fingertips and in the lower abdominal wall. Purpose: to induce a sensation of vigorous breath muscle action and quick inhalation. This aspirate "h" exercise helps produce a feeling for tonal attack and forms a basis for staccato singing.

2.6 *Bubble Slide.* Through gently closed lips, blow enough air to make the lips vibrate, as if you were blowing bubbles under water (or as if you were imitating the sound of a motorcycle). Add vocal tone to make a "bubble slide" like the "hum slide" you learned in chapter 1. (Recall the relaxed, low position of the jaw after yawning; keep the feeling of a loose jaw at all times.) Purpose: to produce tone with a vigorous and steady breath flow through a comfortable pitch range while eliminating tension from the lips.

To find the necessary relaxation for the lips to bubble easily, you may need to hold the outer corners of the mouth with your index fingers, narrowing the vibrating portion. Some students need to substitute the "tongue roll" for lip vibration.

Variations:

a. *Bubble Slide 5th.* Practice this on the same musical interval as "hum slide 5th." (Do you remember "Oh, say"?)
b. *Bubble Slide Rhythm.* When you are comfortable with "bubble slide 5th," do it rhythmically to a count of 4. Count 1: inhale. Count 2: bubble without vocal tone. Count 3: start the upper note and slide down from it. Count 4: finish the slide on the lower note.

2.7   *Tongue Roll Slide.* Do the action of "rolling an rr" with no vocal tone at first, then add tone to make a "tongue roll slide" similar to the "bubble slide." Purpose: to produce tone with a vigorous and steady breath flow through a comfortable pitch range, while eliminating tension in the tongue.

If you have trouble rolling an "r," you are not alone. About 10 percent of English-speaking people have this problem. Learning about a British "flipped r," which is like a quick, light "d," may help you discover the right degree of relaxation to roll the tongue continuously.

This procedure may also help: Silently extend your tongue one-fourth inch out beyond your upper teeth, as if you were going to say "th"; while pulling the tongue back in, whisper "th" very loudly with a rush of air. When the tongue is again inside the teeth, it should start to flap in the moving air-stream. Even two or three flaps count as a success. When this works correctly, you have said "thr" with a flipped or rolled "r." Some British people normally say "three" this way.

If this doesn't work, substitute "bubble slide" for the "tongue roll." (If you can do neither one at first, sing on a soft "oo" in class and keep experimenting with them outside of class.)
Variations:
  a.   *Tongue roll slide 5th.* Like "bubble slide 5th."
  b.   *Tongue roll slide rhythm.* Like "bubble slide rhythm."

2.8   *Starter.* Hum the following rhythm on any comfortable pitch. Use "panting" breath action, but let it be more gentle. "Hm" means that a little breath escapes before the "mm." Purpose: to combine agile breath muscle action with accurate attacks on a single pitch, preparing for the quick breaths often needed in songs.

Variations: Sing the syllables "ha" and "ho."

2.9   *Stepper.* Hum the following pattern, starting on any comfortable pitch. Purpose: to combine agile breath muscle action with the accurate attacks on changing pitches.

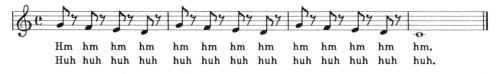

Variations: Sing the syllables "ha" and "ho."

2.10   *Slow Stepper.* Hum the following pattern, starting on any comfortable pitch. Purpose: same as "stepper."

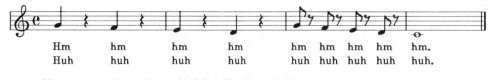

Variations: Sing the syllables "ha" and "ho."

A closing thought   When you sing songs, your mind inevitably goes to the words and notes, and
                        you cannot constantly think of breathing, too. The purpose of practicing at this
                        stage is to make correct breathing action so natural to you that it will continue
                        automatically even when you are not thinking about it. This does not happen
                        right away, so be attentive to your breathing. You may need a lot of practice
                        before correct breath action will continue through a longer note or through a
                        whole phrase. In the meantime, remind yourself often to use correct breath action
                        for the starts of phrases, at least.

Additional reading   *A practical, illustrated book of exercises that will help you stand, sit, and move more efficiently
                             and gracefully:*
                        The Alexander Technique by Sarah Barker. Bantam Books, 1978.

                        *A scientifically sound, detailed, but clear description of the physiology of singing, including pho-
                             tographs of a dissected diaphragm and other vocal organs:*
                        Dynamics of the Singing Voice by Meribeth Bunch. Springer Verlag, 1982.

3 Free Tone

How can I think and talk about vocal tone? How should I start a tone? Stop a tone?

EACH of us has a distinctive natural vocal quality that results from the unique characteristics of a physical vocal instrument, but we can also make many choices about ways of using our voices. When we produce tonal qualities we like, we can choose to use them more often and substitute them for qualities we do not like. In this chapter we will consider various kinds of tone quality, as well as how to start and stop tones.

Tone quality

Think of a voice you like to hear. What words describe the way that voice sounds?

Too often, people answer this question with judgmental words like "pretty" or "beautiful" and stop there. We need a wider vocabulary of words that describe tones we like and don't like; it will help us make decisions about how to improve our own voices.

Here are some words, arranged in contrasting pairs, that voice teachers sometimes use to describe voices.

agile—stiff	crooning—supported	nasal—throaty
breathy—clear	forced—free	somber—bright
even—uneven	dull—resonant	harsh—mellow
lyric—dramatic		strong—weak

Consider what these words mean to you. Do they describe some recorded voices you know? Which words describe your singing right now?

The words just given are not scientific terms, so not everyone agrees when to use them; but all of them relate to vocal technique. Here are other, more subjective words that describe how a voice affects our emotions: timid, bold, irritating, boring, soothing, warm, velvety, brassy, authoritative, ingratiating, shrill.

What words (or other words you may think of) describe the effect that some other persons' voices have on you? What words describe the effect your voice has on other people, or the effect you would like your voice to have on other people?

The science of acoustics explains differences in tone quality in terms of the "overtones" that accompany every musical tone (except an electronically generated sine wave). Briefly, every musical tone consists of a basic pitch, the "fundamental," and also numerous vibrations at higher pitches, known as overtones or "partials." Normally, you are not aware of hearing overtones, but you perceive them in terms of tone colors.

If you sing one pitch while changing the vowel from "ah" to "ee," the fundamental does not change, but the overtones do; you are strengthening some overtones and weakening others. The change takes place automatically in response to your mental image of the vowels you want to sing. This easy, normal process reveals a basic principle: *You will change and develop your vocal quality by imagining the sounds you want.* Any vocal instrument has some limitations, of course, but most of us have far more possibilities than we imagine.

Tonal goals

What are some characteristics of a "good" voice, one that we like to hear?

1. *Audibility.* We want to hear a voice easily in a fair-sized room without a microphone. Anyone can meet this goal. If you practice applying energy to your voice and removing physical tensions, your voice will develop enough carrying power to sing in public. Good teachers agree that a strong tone is a by-product of good vocal habits, not a goal in itself.

2. *Resonance.* A quality of "ring" in the voice results from strong overtones, particularly certain ones at a very high pitch that affect the human ear pleasantly. Even a low male voice requires these high overtones, up around 3,000–3,200 Hz (vibrations per second). A voice without them seems dull, lacking in beauty and carrying power. Again, any healthy voice can develop enough "ring" for good singing.

3. *Clarity.* We prefer a tone with no extra noises (for instance, breathiness). Such noises do not add resonance because they do not vibrate in time with the overtones; we try to eliminate them.

4. *Intelligibility,* which is clarity of consonant and vowel formation. Again, anyone who really cares about communicating with an audience can achieve this. Intelligent application and hard work go into it.

5. *Pure intonation.* Good musicianship requires an ability to start, continue, and stop a tone on pitch, without sliding up or down unintentionally. If you think you might be tone-deaf, look up this topic in chapter 12. Almost all individuals have a good enough musical ear to sing in tune acceptably.

6. *Dynamic variety.* Musical expression requires an ability to sing softer and louder, with smooth changes from one level of dynamics to another. Even a pleasant tone becomes boring without dynamic variety.

7. *Timbral variety.* Dramatic expression requires an ability to change vocal tone-color (timbre), with "bright" tones (stronger high partials) and "dark" tones (weaker high partials) and other qualities produced in response to your imagination and feelings.

8. *Vibrato.* A well-produced voice is capable of a regular, periodic pitch oscillation above and below a basic pitch. More is said about vibrato later in this chapter.

9. *Range.* Most songs require more than an octave (8 scale tones). "The Star-Spangled Banner" requires a twelfth (12 scale tones). A professional singer is expected to sing at least two octaves (15 scale tones) with comfort and good quality, not counting some weaker tones below and above the range that is usable in public performance. In fact, every healthy voice has a range of more than two octaves, needing only the skill and practice to make those tones usable. This is why good teachers agree that range, like loudness, is a by-product of good vocal habits, not a goal in itself.

10. *Ease/freedom.* Good singing takes both mental and physical effort, but the audience doesn't want to know about that. We want to enjoy an unrestrained, spontaneous sound without any evidence of rigid tension. The singer should look, as well as sound, comfortable.

These are the characteristics of a good voice. Your voice may already have one or several of them to a satisfactory degree. Have you found anything in this list that seems impossible for you to develop? Don't worry. Chances are that you can develop all of these qualities in your voice.

Does this mean that anyone can have a career as a great singer? No, of course not. Anyone can swing a baseball bat, but not everyone can play in the major leagues. A great singer possesses all of the basic resources listed above and uses them with superior skill, refinement, and imagination. We can hardly begin to list what goes into a major singing career: years of study; strong musical skills; superior health; vivid personality; artistic creativity; dramatic flair; and much more. Business sense, unflagging ambition, ability to choose the right teachers, coaches, and agents, and, yes, money, are also ingredients in most singing careers. Furthermore, not everyone who could have a singing career wants one enough to live the demanding life of a performer.

But is your voice worth developing? Yes, definitely. You set your own goals and make decisions about the priority that singing has in your life. Your goal may be to sing in a barbershop chorus, to entertain your friends, to sing at worship services, to participate in a community chorus or theater. These are all realizable goals for anyone with a normal healthy voice. Between choral singing and solo stardom there is an infinite number of possibilities for artistic self-expression and satisfaction. With time, work, training, and imagination you may go much further than you foresee right now.

Vibrato

A student who was searching for words asked me, "What do you call it when a voice kind of waves up and down and it's nice?" Answer: Vibrato, one of the qualities we listen for in a voice, whether we realize it or not. Very few voices use vibrato all the time; but when we hear it, we feel that a voice is free and relaxed, warm and expressive.

When we hear a tone with vibrato, we think we are hearing a certain pitch. Actually, we are hearing the voice rise above and fall below the pitch. At the same time, the volume and quality vary as well. Vibrato is such a natural part of a freely produced voice that we are likely to think that a voice without it is "no good."

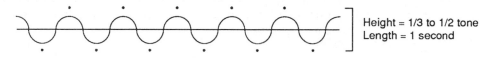

Height = 1/3 to 1/2 tone
Length = 1 second

An attractive vibrato occurs at a rate of six or seven cycles per second. It often carries the tone ¼ tone above and below the basic pitch. As with the other vital attributes of a good voice, almost everyone can develop a pleasing vibrato. (Some individuals have difficulty recognizing vibrato, as music psychologists have found. Even some accomplished singers who have a perfectly normal vibrato are unable to say whether they have one or not.)

Some voices have vibrato from childhood and are never without it. They would do well to experiment with straight tone, deliberately removing the vibrato, primarily by imagining a tone without vibrato. Some conductors may ask you to eliminate vibrato for a particular style, and you need this kind of control.

Other voices could use vibrato, but inhibit it. The following are some reasons I have heard:

> "My teacher said that if I try to use vibrato it will be unnatural; I should wait until I'm older and it will come naturally." False: The vibrato you have in your teens is yours. Use it with pride.

"The choir director said my vibrato made my voice stick out." Translation: One mature voice among a group of immature voices caused a problem that the director didn't know how to solve. It would be better to improve the weaker voices than to stifle the one good voice.

"I don't want my voice to sound 'operatic' and affected." Don't worry, you won't go overboard. Try singing with vibrato and ask your friends if they like it. Also, listen thoughtfully to your favorite singers; you will hear some vibrato in almost any style, not just in opera.

With an attitude change, such students sometimes begin to use vibrato immediately. All they need is to give themselves permission.

If you have never experienced a tone with vibrato, it may take a while before you achieve the right balance of energy and relaxation to allow vibrato to occur spontaneously. When you hear vibrato come into the voice on any single tone, take notice of it and encourage it to reappear.

Singers use vibrato differently in different styles; some country singers seldom use it, while some gospel and blues singers use more than a half-tone. Jazz stylists, particularly, add and subtract vibrato at will as part of their expressive technique.

Sometimes we hear a vibrato that is too wide, too fast, or too slow, or one that pulses loud and soft like a bleat. Like too much of any good thing, all such excesses are unpleasant. We use the word *tremolo* to describe any of them. Tremolos can usually be corrected by improving breath support and learning the right balance of vitality and relaxation in singing.

Attack and release

The start of a musical tone is commonly called the "attack." A truly free and resonant tonal attack is "half the battle." If an attack is shaky or out of tune, the whole phrase is likely to bog down or to end flat. Likewise, a tone quality that is harsh and tense on the attack is likely to remain tense to the end of the phrase. Aim for a free, clear, effortless tone on the attack.

The first and most important advice regarding the attack is to imagine the tone—the pitch, quality, and dynamic level—before you sing it. A good attack starts with a mental impulse put into action by the breath, not by the throat.

"Release" is the ending of a musical tone. Again, a correct release results from a mental decision to stop or reverse the flow of breath. When we sing one phrase after another, each release is simultaneous with taking air in for the coming phrase.

Three facts about the vocal cords

Moving air causes a tone by vibrating the vocal cords. Chapter 11 describes the vocal cords in some detail, but at this point you need to know three things about them.

1. The vocal cords can be brought together over the windpipe, closing it so tightly that no air can enter or leave the lungs.
2. They are drawn apart when we breathe in and out normally, allowing air to pass between them.
3. They come together during singing, but loosely enough so that air can pass between them and make them vibrate.

These three facts give us a basis for understanding the three methods of attack: glottal, breathy, and clean.

Three methods of attack

1. *Glottal attack* occurs when the vocal cords are held closed and air blows them apart to start the tone. (The word "glottal" comes from *glottis*, the opening between the cords. Admittedly, the expression "glottal attack" is

illogical, but it is widely used by speech and singing teachers.) The resulting sound is explosive and coughlike; sometimes it is noticeably noisy, sometimes quiet, barely audible.

One of the main functions of the vocal cords is to close off the windpipe when it is necessary to pressurize the air in the lungs. Many people do this when exerting the upper body, as in lifting a heavy weight or chopping wood. High pressure on the vocal cords and the hard friction between them can cause wear and tear, such as you experience when you cough too much. For this reason you should learn to exercise without holding your breath. (Weight lifters have a good maxim: "Blow the weight up.")

Similarly, some people habitually speak with "glottal stops," closing the vocal cords before every word that begins with a vowel and blowing the cords open every time with a little coughing sound. This abuses the vocal cords, as all speech therapists agree. Clearly, we must avoid this kind of attack in singing.

2. *Breathy attack* occurs when air passes between the vocal cords before they meet and begin vibrating. This happens every time we say the consonant "h." Breathy attack is OK, providing it is intentional. In fact, the voice exercises in chapter 2 all began with *h*, in order to be sure of avoiding glottal attacks.

Two problems sometimes go with breathy attack: "ha-ha" or unintentional *h*, which is easily corrected by simple awareness, and "scooping" or attacking the pitch from below, which is also cured by having a clear concept of the desired tone.

3. *Clean attack* occurs when the movement of air and the closure of the vocal cords are practically simultaneous. Fortunately, the body coordinates this delicate adjustment automatically if we have a clear mental concept of the desired tone.

Three methods of release

Review the three facts that we learned about the vocal cords. Just as they implied three methods of attack, they also imply that there are three ways of releasing a tone.

1. *Stopped release.* The vocal cords close together tightly, ending the tone but also preventing any intake of breath. This causes unnecessary friction between the edges of the cords and delays a natural preparation to continue singing.

2. *Breathy release.* The vocal cords separate, correctly ending the tone, but extra air flows outward, perhaps audibly. The outward flow delays our preparation to continue singing and perhaps makes an unwanted noise.

3. *Clean release.* The diaphragm drops, the vocal cords separate, and air flows into the lungs simultaneously.

Obviously, the only desirable release is the "clean" one, in which the ending of one tone simultaneously begins the preparation for the next.

How to vocalize

Repeat the exercises from chapters 1 and 2. Each chapter adds to your repertoire of exercises that help you get ready to sing every day, whether or not you feel inspired. Especially, repeat "abdominal action," "rib-widening," and "full breath action" until you feel confident that you breathe correctly for singing at any time, at will. Repeat the voice exercises with added awareness of attack and release.

Here is some advice to help you get your best tone in the next exercises.

1. Use a hummed consonant, *n* or *m*, to prepare a resonant intensity for the tone.

2. Test your hum to be sure that you do not use a harmful glottal attack. Stop both ears with your fingers, then hum a tone in easy range. If there is a glottal attack, you will hear and feel the click or coughlike attack. To change this habit, temporarily start each tone with a "silent h," a little breath that escapes ahead of the tone. This will replace a harmful habit with a harmless one, a slightly breathy attack, which you can easily drop when you no longer need it.

3. Endeavor to carry the humming intensity of *n* or *m* into *Uh*, a neutral vowel that is formed with a uniformly open vocal passage. Think of *Uh* as a free and ringing tone (Up!), never muffled (Dull!) in tonal character.

4. Use *Uh*, with its free, open-throated feeling, as the basis for other vowels. Transitions from *n* to *Uh* to *Oh* or *Ah* should be smooth and flowing, with no feeling of changing resonance space.

5. Use a vital and comfortable tone with a medium dynamic level, either medium loud (mf) or medium soft (mp).

6. Start each exercise on a comfortable pitch somewhat above your normal speaking pitch. Sing it twice or more, noticing how it improves with repetition; then transpose it downward several times to lower keys. Repeat the exercise on a somewhat higher pitch and again transpose downward several times. Repeat a key whenever you feel you can improve the tone. Start over again in a higher key, if you can do so easily, without a sense of reaching or straining. This is a strategy for exploring your higher range with ease. "Take what the voice gives you," as voice teacher Oren Brown expresses it, rather than force the voice to sing a wider range.

When you can attack a tone perfectly and release it just as well, then sustaining the tone is simply a matter of continuing the breath flow. You have already sustained moderately long tones in the "starter," "stepper," and "slow stepper" exercises in Chapter 2. Now you can do similar exercises and gradually lengthen the time you can sustain a steady tone.

Exercises

The first new exercises, 3.1 through 3.5, deal with the clean attack as we usually use it in normal, smoothly connected singing. Purpose: to produce a free, efficient, uniform tone with clean attack and release in various musical situations.

3.1 *Hummer #1.*   **3.2** *Hummer #2.*

3.3 *Quick Hummer.*   **3.4** *Down Five.*

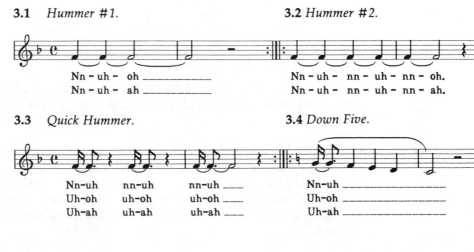

3.5 *Singles.*

Nn - uh - oh,   nn - uh - oh,   nn - uh - oh,   nn - uh - oh.
Uh - oh - ah,   uh - oh - ah,   uh - oh - ah,   uh - oh - ah.

3.6 *Antiscoop.* "Scooping" is the bad habit of starting a tone under pitch and tuning it up while singing it. Beginners sometimes do this because they are used to speaking at a pitch much lower than their singing range. Sing this with the small grace notes sounded definitely at first and then so rapidly that they aren't heard, although still in mind as an approach from above. Purpose: to approach the tone mentally from above and avoid the temptation to scoop.

Nn-uh,   nn-uh,   nn-uh,   nn-uh,   nn-uh,   nn-uh,   nn-uh.
Nn-oh,   nn-oh,   nn-oh,   nn-oh,   nn-oh,   nn-oh,   nn-oh.
Uh-oh,   uh-oh,   uh-oh,   uh-oh,   uh-oh,   uh-oh,   uh-oh.

3.7 *Tune-up.* Sing the quick syllables lightly, pronouncing *m*'s and *n*'s quickly. Keep the jaw out of action as much as possible. Sing each measure two or three times without stopping for breath. In voice classes, sing in two parts. Purpose: to prepare for sustaining long tones with continued vitality and freshness.

Mee- meh- mah- moh- moo.   Mee- meh- mah- moh- moo.
Nee- neh- nah- noh- noo.   Nee- neh- nah - noh - noo.

The remaining exercises deal with the quick impulses needed for clean attack and release in staccato singing. *Staccato* is Italian for "detached," and staccato passages are sung by sudden attacks and releases of each note. As a general rule, each staccato note should be followed by a rest as long or longer than the note is sustained.

At first, staccatos can be practiced on "Hah" to prevent glottal attacks and stopped releases. Later, think of renewing the vowel for each note with a definite breath impulse, omitting the actual *h*. Sing lightly, with attention to attacking and releasing cleanly and in tune. Do not take breath between staccato notes until the end of the exercise. (In "Starter," exercise 2.7, you took small breaths between the detached notes.)

3.8 *Staccato Attack.* Notice that the two versions of this exercise, a and b, sound exactly alike. Purpose: to develop the light, quick attacks and releases of staccato style.

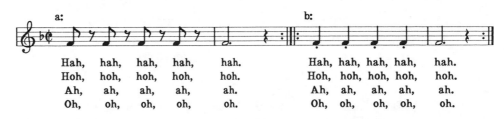

Hah,   hah,   hah,   hah,   hah.   Hah, hah, hah, hah,   hah.
Hoh,   hoh,   hoh,   hoh,   hoh.   Hoh, hoh, hoh, hoh,   hoh.
Ah,   ah,   ah,   ah,   ah.   Ah, ah, ah, ah,   ah.
Oh,   oh,   oh,   oh,   oh.   Oh, oh, oh, oh,   oh.

3.9 *Staccato Scale.* Purpose: same as #8.

Hah, hah, hah, hah,   hah.   Hah, hah, hah, hah,   hah.
Hoh, hoh, hoh, hoh,   hoh.   Hoh, hoh, hoh. hoh,   hoh.
Ah, ah, ah, ah,   ah.   Ah, ah, ah, ah,   ah.
Oh, oh, oh, oh,   oh.   Oh, oh, oh, oh,   oh.

Additional listening   *If you want to expand your ideas about tone quality, listen to recordings of singing styles that are unfamiliar to you. Some examples might be: Italian opera, Native American songs, Beijing opera, Renaissance music using a countertenor voice, Wagnerian opera, music from India, 1930s jazz and blues, and various pop styles. Examples should be available in any public library listening area.*

4 Changing Resonances in Your Voice

Guiding questions: *Why does the upper part of my voice sound and feel different from the lower part? What kinds of voices are there and what kind do I have? How can I make my voice more resonant?*

HAVE you noticed that some parts of your voice feel different from others? Are there some notes that you can sing in more than one way? Untrained singers often feel uncomfortable about inconsistencies found between their low and high notes. Let's learn about them and decide how to work with them.

Chest or head?

Try this experiment: place your hands on your ribs and sing the lowest note you can imagine. What do you feel? You probably feel vibrations in your bones. Now keep your hands on your ribs and sing a high, light note. Do you still feel the vibrations? Now start on a high note and let the pitch slide downward. As the pitch goes down, you will reach a pitch where you feel the ribs begin to vibrate again.

Centuries ago singers noticed these sensations. Not knowing about the larynx, they thought that certain tones really originated in the chest and others in the head. This is not true—chest vibration is simply a response to tone, a sympathetic vibration. However, many singers still speak of chest voice and head voice because of the familiar sensations that accompany our low and high registers.

Luckily for us, our voices have many qualities available, not just two. When we imagine tones, our vocal cords adjust themselves subtly, changing in length, in thickness, in shape, and in the amount of contact between them. We don't just flick a switch to turn on the chest voice or turn on the head voice. Good singers continually mix and blend their tones when they decide how loud or soft to sing and what quality to use.

Because our vocal cords are hidden from sight and respond chiefly to mental images of tone, voice teachers differ in the ways they speak about the different areas of the voice. Most teachers of classical music want to train a voice so that all notes are equal in quality and strength. They might speak of one register, meaning that the highest and lowest notes and all the notes in between sound alike.

Some teachers speak of a one-register voice that is either a rare gift of nature or an end product of years of training. Some believe that a one-register voice is an illusion that a skilled singer gives to an audience. However that may be, most students have unequal tones in their voices and are well aware of them.

A majority of singers are aware of three registers:

1. head or light mechanism;
2. medium or blended mechanism; and
3. chest or heavy mechanism.

Three registers were recognized in the 1840s by Manuel Garcia II, the first person who ever used a dental mirror to observe the vocal cords in motion. In *Hints on Singing* he offered this classic definition: "A register is a series of consecutive homogeneous sounds produced by one mechanism. . . ."

Various theories of registers have been presented. The late Dr. R. Berton Coffin, while agreeing that vocal cords act differently in various registers, showed that there are also acoustical distinctions between them. Coffin identified 11 registers, of which the lowest ones are used only by basses and the highest ones are used only by sopranos.

These differing theories still have some common ground:

1. Men do most of their singing in the chest voice, blending to the medium and head for their higher notes.

2. Women do most of their singing in the head voice, blending to medium and chest for their lower notes.

3. The registers overlap a great deal, allowing us to make choices according to the vowel, tone quality, and loudness desired.

Your choice

Which register do you like to use when you sing? Which is your strongest?

Let's start by thinking about your speaking voice. Is it high or low? Our modern American culture strongly prefers low speaking voices. Parents admonish children to keep their voices down. Girls may or may not notice that their voices drop by four or five notes during puberty, but they definitely feel more grown-up when their voices lose the squeakiness of childhood. Adolescent boys can't help but notice that their voices drop an octave or more, and their friends and family praise them for sounding like men. Many of us, whether female or male, respond to positive responses from the people around us by speaking as low as we can and even forcing our voices to go lower than is really comfortable.

Are you curious to know the pitch of your speaking voice? (Your teacher may need to help with this experiment.) Speak a syllable that you can hold naturally and strike a note on the piano that matches the pitch of your speaking voice. You may be surprised at how low it is. Many women speak below middle C, even though they sing much higher.

What is the best pitch for speaking? Speech teachers recommend that you use a habitual pitch about one-third of the way up the scale from your lowest possible speaking tone to your highest. Observe your speaking pitch over a period of several days, noticing how high your voice goes when you are excited or surprised. Notice also whether you use a high pitch or a low pitch when you laugh or cough. Eventually, with your teacher's help, you can find your most comfortable pitch level for speaking. Because it varies with expression, it is not necessary to measure it exactly.

Does speaking too low or too high cause any problems? Yes, it can cause vocal fatigue and even voice loss. Also, our wish to speak low means that many persons start out singing in the heavy voice and feel uncomfortable about experimenting with the blended and light voices. Of course, the opposite can also be true, and some students need encouragement to use the strength that the heavy voice will give to their low notes.

Your voice teacher will assess what part of your voice is strongest and will encourage you to work on strengthening the weaker parts. A basic goal of voice training is to balance and strengthen all of the notes in your range.

What kind of voice?

What kind of voice do you like to hear? Wouldn't it be lucky if your own voice turned out to be the kind you like most? Some people are that lucky, maybe because they instinctively like voices that resemble their own.

You may be asking yourself, "What kind of voice do I have?" Your voice teacher may answer that question right away, or your teacher may prefer to wait and see how your voice develops over a period of time. A choral director classifies voices quickly in auditions, but voice teachers prefer to take more time.

Poor vocal habits and wrong ideas about singing can hide the natural quality of your voice, and it may take weeks or months for it to emerge. Some voice students imitate a favorite singer whose quality is not at all like their own. They are not deliberately faking; they simply think that their favorite singer's style is the best way to sing.

Imitation is a valid way of learning to sing, but only if the sound you imitate is right for you. You are studying voice because you want to change and expand your voice, but if you try to change your voice permanently into something that is against its physical nature, you will seriously limit it, perhaps even lose it. There are serious risks, for instance, if a woman, to help out her choir, sings tenor all the time. If you use one part of your range exclusively, you run a risk of overusing it and making the rest of your voice seem feeble by comparison. A good way to use your voice is to balance the use of the registers.

Voice types

To answer the question "What kind of voice do I have?" you need to know what names are given to different voices. This becomes a little confusing because voices have somewhat different names in different kinds of music.

Choral music uses four kinds of voices: soprano, alto, tenor, and bass. If the music divides into more than four parts, any section can divide into higher and lower voices, for instance, first altos and second altos (abbreviated Alto I and Alto II).

Opera requires more precise classifications of voices. Sopranos who love to sing far above the staff are called coloratura or lyric-coloratura sopranos. Lower-voiced women are divided into mezzo-sopranos, who sing almost as high as sopranos, and contraltos, who specialize in singing low. Lower-voiced men are similarly divided into baritones, bass-baritones, and basses. In addition, operatic voices can be further classified by words that describe what the voice does best or how it sounds, such as lyric or dramatic. Opera fans love to argue over what kind of voice is best for a certain role, based on their own interpretation of the character.

Broadway musical theater uses a different concept in classifying women's voices. Most roles require a woman to "belt," which means to sing at a high energy level, especially in a low range. Some belting roles go even lower than an operatic contralto. A blended or head tone is called "legitimate" or just "legit" on Broadway. A casting notice might read: "Must sing both belt and legit." The Broadway concept is that belt and legit are ways of singing that a woman chooses according to her natural ability, training and personal preference. (Probably male voices also belt, but the contrast between belt and legit is less striking in male voices because of the prevalence of chest tone at all times.)

Table 4.1.
Types of voices

	Choral	Operatic/Concert	Pop/Broadway
WOMEN			
(high)		Coloratura Soprano	
	Soprano	Soprano	Legit/soprano
	Alto	Mezzo-soprano	Belt
(low)		Contralto	
MEN			
(high)	Tenor	Tenor	Tenor
		Baritone	
	Bass	Bass-baritone	Baritone
(low)		Bass	

Belt and pop singing

Is belting dangerous? Many voice teachers think so. It is especially dangerous for young voices because their muscular development is not complete. Other voice teachers may reject belting because they simply do not like the sound. Yet, if you accept a role in a musical, you may have to do some belting.

Certainly, belting is a high-energy way of singing and carries some risks, just like other high-energy activities, including singing opera or playing hockey. Some women belt well and sing professionally on Broadway for years without losing their voices. Others belt poorly, ignore trouble signs such as hoarseness and pain, and lose their voices in short order.

The same goes for both women and men who sing rock, jazz, or other kinds of popular music. Loud electronic instruments cause many young singers to force their voices and even lose them.

If you do popular or Broadway music, please don't keep it a secret because you expect your teacher to disapprove. On the contrary, your teacher can help you sing it without hurting yourself.

Finding your best resonance

Resonance means the strengthening of a tone through sympathetic vibration, which is *the tendency of air in an enclosed or partially enclosed space to vibrate in response to a musical tone.* For example, the tone of a vibrating guitar string is strengthened by vibrations of the air inside the body of the guitar, and the tone made by the vibrating lips of a trumpeter is strengthened by vibrations of the air inside the horn.

Just as tone resonates inside a guitar or trumpet, the tone made by your vocal cords resonates in your throat, mouth, and nose. While making your voice louder, resonance also changes the proportions between the various overtones that give your voice both its basic quality and vowel color. The overtones change because of changes in the shape and size of your throat and mouth openings.

In time you will learn to feel resonance in your vocal instrument and to judge when you have your best resonance. Your teacher is your best ally in this important process.

Criteria for your own singing

Here are some questions to help you decide what tone quality is best for you. Your mental concepts about singing are developing quickly, and you can rely on the two senses that control singing, *feeling* and *hearing,* to know when you are on the right track.

How tonal production should feel

1. *Is the tone easy and relaxed in the throat?* If you feel tension, pressure, or pain in your throat, there is clearly something wrong.

2. *Is there a feeling that the tone can be manipulated up or down in range, louder or softer in dynamics, darker or brighter in tone color?*
   A lack of flexibility in these three respects is a strong sign of unwanted tension.

How tonal production should sound

1. *Is the tone smooth, steady, and flowing, with an even vibrato?*
2. *Is the tone ringing, intense ("hummy"), and efficient in resonance?*
3. *Is the vowel clear and pure?*
4. *Is the tone on pitch?*

Increasing your resonance

With the guidelines you have just read, you can safely begin to strengthen your resonance. Stronger resonance means that your voice has more carrying power, more ability to seize and hold the attention of a listener, more power to communicate your feelings.

Do you remember hearing a baby's cry? It instantly grabs your attention and doesn't let go. Other powerful communicators are laughs, groans, whimpers, and sighs. These are all wordless emotional messages, and our brains instinctively give them attention. Singing takes some of the emotional power of these natural sounds, gives them musical form, and combines them with words. This understanding of the nature of singing gives us clues to discovering our best resonance.

Resonance arises instinctively when we

- really want to communicate;
- use emotional energy and enthusiasm;
- put physical energy into our sound;
- get rid of physical and emotional blocks.

Experiment with the sentences that follow, speaking them out loud. Use enough energy to be heard in a large room. See how many different emotional meanings you can give to each one.

- Will you sing a solo?
- You should have been there!
- So you are the one!
- Was there ever any other one?
- Hey you, get away from my car!

Can you make up other sentences that call up emotional responses? At this stage, let your feelings be the key to vocal resonance. The exercises that follow will help you get rid of physical tensions that interfere with resonance; later, in the chapter on vowels, you will learn more about the technical side of resonance.

Relaxation and resonance

Your best resonance usually goes along with a sense of freedom and relaxation. Tension in the face, tongue, jaw muscles, and neck, which are areas closely adjacent to the larynx itself, will immediately impair ease, quality, and control of singing. Other muscles less closely involved, such as those in the hands and shoulders, will also interfere sooner or later if allowed to become tense. In a healthy throat, if the extrinsic (outer) muscles are relaxed, the intrinsic muscles of the larynx will usually function normally.

Exercises

The next exercises continue the process begun in chapter 1, eliminating physical tensions that may interfere with resonant vocal production. While not everyone has the same tensions, all of these exercises are good procedures for warming up the voice. Combine them with the physical exercises from chapters 1 and 2.

4.1 *Mental Messages.* Imagine the muscles of the cheekbones under the eyes completely relaxed, the lips loose, the tongue lying forward in the mouth, and the jaw hanging freely. One by one, send mental messages to the cheeks, lips, tongue, and jaw to relax. (If you later sing any tone that feels strained, the best single advice that can be given to free the tone is to imagine complete relaxation of the flesh over the cheekbones.)

4.2 *Jaw Wobble.* Open your mouth, place your hands on both sides of your jaw, and then move your jaw *gently* from side to side. The hands supply the movement, not the jaw muscles, which should be perfectly loose. If you cannot do this, work patiently with a mirror until you discover how to release the muscles that are holding the jaw stiff. (If you know you have temporo-mandibular joint, "TMJ," problems or if this exercise causes discomfort, skip it and consult your dentist.)

4.3 *Jaw Flopper.* Shake your head easily from side to side, with the jaw and lips swinging loosely from side to side.

4.4 *Yes Nod.* Nod your head lazily up and down to relax your neck muscles. (Don't worry about looking silly; you are working to achieve needed relaxation.)

4.5 *Hand Shake.* Shake your hands loosely from the wrists, dispelling any tension in your arms.

4.6 *Sigh.* Take several deep, gentle, sighlike breaths, relaxing the upper body on each exhalation with a sudden "let-go" feeling.

Let your voice warm up on some of the vocal exercises from chapters 1 through 3 before going on to the next exercises. Pay special attention to exercise 3.5, "Singles," because it covers a full octave. Do you have a better understanding now of why the high tones feel different from the low tones?

4.7 *Syllabic Singles.* Purpose: to gain comfort on notes far apart in the scale, using syllables to name the notes for greater musical awareness and pitch accuracy. Transpose up and down to other comfortable keys. (The syllables for the complete scale are presented in the next chapter.)

Do, _____   so, _____   do, _____   so. _____

4.8 *Little Arches.* Even before you sing the first note, have the first *two* notes of each phrase in mind. If you do this, the upward jump will be in tune and the tones will connect smoothly. Purpose: to use breath and resonance evenly in a small melodic pattern. (High voices: Sing this in F Major, starting on b♭.)

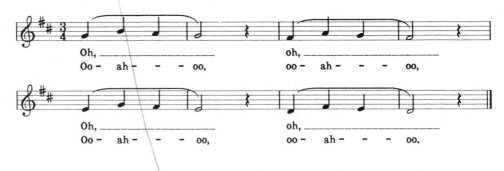

Oh, _____   oh, _____
Oo - ah - - - oo,   oo - ah - - - oo,

Oh, _____   oh, _____
Oo - ah - - - oo,   oo - ah - - - oo.

4.9 *Octave Flip.* Start on any high, light note that comes easily to your voice. "Flip" to the low note and back up, that is, change pitches suddenly, allowing the clicking sound that one hears in yodelling. Transpose downward by half-steps a few times, then start over on a higher pitch. Purpose: to sense a contrast between the light and heavy registers in their pure forms, not mixed.

4.10 *Octave Sigh.* Start on any high, light note that comes easily to your voice. Sing the word "sigh" and also feel that you really are sighing while your voice slides down one octave, passing through all of the notes without stopping on any. Begin the slide on the third beat of the measure. Transpose downward by half-steps a few times, then start over on a higher pitch. Purpose: to smooth out and minimize the differences between the light and heavy registers, mixing them gradually on the way down.

4.11 *5-Note Bee-dee's.* Start on any easy note around the mid-point of your range. Transpose downward to your lowest comfortable range. Purpose: to sense an easy, bright resonance, combined with quick, light articulation.

4.12 *5-Note Ee-Ah's.* Start on any easy note around the mid-point of your range. Sense the brightness of the first vowel and let the brightness carry into the second vowel. Purpose: to sense the way one vowel can brighten another. Transpose downward to your lowest comfortable range, then start over again a little higher.

4.13 *Focusers.* Try these combinations of syllables, which have been used by many singers to "center" their vocal energy. With your teacher's guidance, notice which ones work best for you and add them to your daily exercise. Purpose: to experience the relationship between vowel and resonance, as well as the role of initial consonants in preparing tone. Transpose into several comfortable keys.

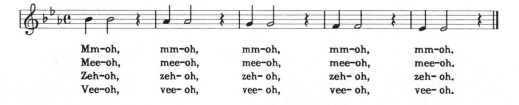

Additional reading   *To learn more about all kinds of voices, both nonoperatic and operatic:*
The Singing Voice by Robert Rushmore. Dembner Books (W. W. Norton), 2nd Edition, 1984.

For more of the technique and style of pop singing:
Born to Sing by Elisabeth Howard and Howard Austin. Vocal Power, 18653 Ventura Blvd.,
Suite 551-J, Tarzana, CA, 91356, 1989.

5 Preparing a Song

Guiding questions: *What is the best way to learn the words and music of songs so that I can sing them expressively and confidently?*

EVEN though there is much more to learn about vocal technique, you can begin to use what you know in songs. This book contains a large variety of songs that are within your range, songs that will provide you with fun, as well as an opportunity to improve and learn more about your voice and about singing.

The first two steps

Naturally, the first step in learning a song is to *choose* one. That seems too obvious to mention, but many beginners are not sure how to make a choice. Your teacher may choose your first song for you; but if you were on your own, you could use the following bit of advice.

1. *Choose words that you can believe in.* If words don't make sense to you, they are harder to learn, and it is harder to motivate yourself to sing expressively.

2. *Choose an easy song* and do it well, rather than a hard song that you can't finish. If all your energy goes into learning difficult rhythms or rapid-fire words, you can't give much thought to improving your tone quality.

3. *Choose a short song* over a longer one. At first, you will learn more by doing several short songs than by sticking to one long one. Also, your teacher can give you more help in lessons if you sing a short song several times rather than a long song once.

After you have done several easy songs the time will come to apply your skill to longer, more challenging songs. Now the main goal is to learn, quickly and pleasurably, how to sing.

In order to be sure you like the chosen song, you will want to *hear it* right away. Use your cassette recorder to tape the song in class. You can sing through some or all of the song, but only as long as it is easy and fun to do so. Let any hard parts wait until later.

The next step comes naturally if you have a positive attitude: *identify something you really like* in your song. Make a mental note of it. As you spend hours on your song, you will want to remember why you liked it in the first place and why others may enjoy hearing it, too. Does it appeal to you because of a mood, a mental picture, or an idea? Because of a graceful melody or a lively rhythm? Because of its quaintness or its modern sound?

Learning the words

You have made friends with your new song—why not start singing it? Simply because you don't want to make mistakes that will turn into habits. Also, singing in an insecure, uncertain way brings on tension that can turn into bad vocal habits.

Patient work now will pay off in confidence and success when we are ready to perform. To demonstrate the process of learning a song, we will study "When Laura Smiles," found on page 128 of this book. We will go into enough detail to show the kinds of preparation that will help you with any song you want to sing.

Try to hear "When Laura Smiles" at least once and catch some feature about it that you like, perhaps the lively tempo or the playful downward scales on the words "smiles" and "revives."

A wise person once said that *all* songs are love songs, and there's no doubt about this case. "When Laura Smiles" is a love song written by a man about a woman, but any man can sing it about any woman. (By historical custom, a man can preserve the privacy of his beloved by singing to her under a false name.) Also, the song is so graceful and charming that no one would mind hearing a woman sing it. (She might be helping out some poor man who can't sing for himself!)

Starting at this point, there are seven steps that we will use to learn "When Laura Smiles." We will begin with the poetry. Do you like poetry? If you're not sure, at least keep an open mind. Every song begins life as a poem. Without words, how could we express what we want to sing about?

(Step 1) *Write out the poem by hand.* Why? When words are spread out under the notes of a melody, you can't see clearly how they fit together to form a poem and tell a story. By writing the words in stanza form, you discover how many lines the poem has and which lines rhyme; later on, this information will help you memorize the words. If you find misprints or wrong punctuations (we hope not!), correct them now before they lead you astray. Here is "When Laura Smiles."

When Laura smiles, her sight revives both night and day.
The earth and heaven views with delight her wanton play,
And her speech with ever flowing music doth repair
The cruel wounds of sorrow and untamed despair.

Love hath no fire but what he steals from her bright eyes.
Time hath no power but that which in her pleasure lies,
For she with her divine beauties all the world subdues,
And fills with heavenly spirits my humble muse.

Of course, this is not everyday language. Philip Rosseter wrote both the words and the music and published them in 1601. Jamestown, Virginia, had not been settled yet; Elizabeth I ruled England; and Shakespeare was writing his plays. Draw on what you know about the Elizabethan period to help you understand the poem.

Your dictionary is a good friend. No one knows every word in the English language, and even a current Broadway lyric might have expressions that you haven't heard before. The dictionary tells us that all of the words in "When Laura Smiles" are current. Only one word has changed its meaning: "wanton" has immoral connotations now, but in Rosseter's time it could mean simply "frolicsome, playful." "Views" in line 2 sounds grammatically incorrect, but Rosseter wrote it that way. Do you want to keep it as it is or change it to "view"? Your decision!

Do you understand everything the poem says? A good test is to (Step 2) *Paraphrase it and summarize its key meaning.* That means that you write the poem out again in your own words and then decide what main message the poet wanted to convey. This time write in prose, because the rhymes and rhythms don't matter, only the meaning. Change as many words as you can without changing the meaning.

Here's a paraphrase, but why don't you try your own version before you read this one? After all, a poetic phrase can have more than one meaning, and yours may mean more to you.

> "Whenever Laura beams, the sight of her cheers up the time of day, whether it is dark or light. All the universe happily watches her frolicsome activities, and her speaking voice is so musical that it heals my badly hurt feelings of sadness and my wild feelings of hopelessness.
>
> "Cupid (a name Love uses when assuming a male form) gets all of his energy from her shining eyes. She has power over Time, making it pass quickly or slowly according to her wish, because her goddess-like charms have power to overcome everything known. And she gives supernatural inspiration to my quite ordinary poetic talent."

Some poems might be difficult to summarize, but this one comes down to "I love Laura!"

Can you see how paraphrasing a poem helps you discover your own feelings about it? Two things should be noted about paraphrasing poetry:

1. A paraphrase is usually longer than the poem because a good poem is concentrated into as few words as possible.

2. No paraphrase says everything that the poem says because a good poem communicates on more than one level, including the musical effects of rhythm and rhyme.

So a poem can mean more than one thing. How do you know your interpretation is right? Talk it through with someone else. Are all interpretations equally right? No. Some are better than others; some are dead wrong. For instance, take the phrase "ever flowing music." Is this sarcasm about Laura's constant talking? Not likely! This poet is too much in love to complain about anything.

Once the meaning is clear, (Step 3) *Read the poem aloud with expression, phrasing, and accentuation.*

Find the words that communicate action and feeling because those words will give the song *expression.* "Smiles," "revives," and "delight" are energy words.

Find the *phrasing* because your breathing will depend on it when you sing. For instance, notice the strong pull of the words "repair the cruel wounds. . . ." A good actor would connect those words in spite of the line-ending.

Notice the correct *accentuation* of the poem because it may give you clues about the musical rhythm. We will come back to this point when we study the music.

Learning the music

Now that you know a lot about the poem, let's combine it with the rhythm of the song. If you read notes already, this part is easy. If you haven't learned to read notes, this would be a good time to read chapter 12, "Notes for Nonmusicians." In the meantime, you will learn the song by ear in class.

Rhythm

Notice that "When Laura Smiles" is written in triple meter, which means an overall rhythmic pattern of three beats per measure. Sit down at a table with the song in front of you. Tap the meter on the tabletop with one hand or both.

Tap the three beats this way: beat 1 near the book, another beat a few inches away, and a third beat further away. At the end of each measure your hand returns from beat 3 position to beat 1 position; its movement through the air gives extra energy to beat 1. If you use both hands, they move away from your body during the 3-beat measure and toward your body after beat 3 to prepare for beat 1. Don't tap all the beats in one spot, because you may lose track of which beat is which.

Now (Step 4) *speak the poem aloud rhythmically, breathing at the right times,* while your hands tap the meter. Use a little higher speaking pitch than usual because your singing voice is probably even higher. Let your voice sound alive and loving, not bored and grumbling.

In the first measure (abbreviated "m1") there is one syllable to each tap of your hand, but in m2 the word "smiles" lasts through three taps. For now you only need to know how the words fit into the meter (the overall beat); disregard the fact that "smiles" and some other words have more than one note per syllable.

tap	tap	tap	tap	tap	tap	tap	tap
1	2	3	1	2	3	1	2
When	Lau-	ra	smiles,--------			her	sight, etc.

You might feel a little conflict already between the rhythm of the music and the words. When you first read the poem, its rhythm went this way:

When Láura smíles, her síght revíves both níght and dáy.

But now as you speak in rhythm, the strong syllables are sometimes on beat 1 and sometimes on beat 2. Elizabethan musicians liked rhythmic shifts like this and used them to keep their music lively.

There is another kind of rhythmic shift in m9–m10, where the second syllable of "ever" lasts through two taps, beat 3 and beat 1. This rhythm may take extra practice.

tap	tap	tap	tap	tap	tap	tap	tap	tap
1	2	3	1	2	3	1	2	3
ev-	- -	er-	- -	flow-	ing	mu-	- -	sic

Work through the whole song, both stanzas, taking time to do this stage correctly. Go slowly enough to keep the rhythms clear, accurate, and easy. By speaking the rhythms, you form vocal habits and breathing habits that will make the song easier when you are ready to sing it. You are also training your eye to move along the line of words, reading just ahead of the word that you are saying in rhythm.

Phrasing

When can you breathe? It looks as though every measure is filled up with notes, and there is no time to breathe. It's up to you to make time. Go back to speaking the poem naturally; wherever you can breathe while speaking the poem, you can breathe when you sing it. Just shorten the note before the breath so that you can breathe and still say the following word on time.

Breathing points can be indicated in your songs with two written signs, a wedge ($\vee$) and a bold comma (,). A comma above the staff means "must breathe." The wedge means "may breathe if you like." If a song has different breathing points in the second stanza, these signs will be printed with the words instead of the music.

Catch breaths At the end of m2 there is a comma, and the next good chance to breathe comes at the end of m6. What should you do? One breathing spot comes before you need it, and the other comes a little late.

In this case, you need a small breath, called a "catch breath," after "smiles." This renews your air supply and makes it easy to sing to the end of m6.

Do you still practice "Starter" (exercise 2.8)? You learned to take small amounts of breath using the correct physical action, and now is the time to use that skill. Here is how you make time for the catch breath:

Later in the song, remember that there can be no breath after "repair." The singer must choose whether to take a catch breath after "wounds" or after "sorrow." In your opinion, which breath interrupts the meaning of the poem less? The choice is yours.

When you practice the second stanza, will you breathe in all of the same places? Not necessarily. Always breathe so that the words make sense.

When you have all the rhythms and breathing points worked out, play your audiocassette of the accompaniment while you speak the poem in rhythm. You're almost ready to sing, but do this step first. When you can speak your poem exactly in rhythm with the recorded accompaniment, you can be satisfied that you really understand the rhythm of your song.

We have gone into a lot of detail about rhythm, with a risk of making it seem more complicated than it really is. Experience shows that most students have rhythmic problems that reduce their confidence in singing. You can work out such problems on your own if you know some of these techniques.

Melody

When you have mastered the words and the rhythms, you are practically singing the song. Next, (Step 5) *learn the melody by ear.*

Play the melody on the piano, or have someone else record it so that you can hear it over and over. Only when the pitches are familiar to your ear can you sing the melody spontaneously.

(Step 6) *Vocalize the melody until you can sing it smoothly.* By "vocalizing" we mean singing on vowels or on nonsense syllables made of both vowels and consonants. People usually try "la-la," but other syllables may work better for you: "Da-da," "loo-loo," "bay-bay," and "thaw-thaw" are good possibilities. Pairs of contrasting syllables are also good, such as "zoo-me-zoo-me" or "day-blah-day-blah," sung over and over.

Why vocalize a song? So that you concentrate on the melody, learning to sing it smoothly and comfortably. If certain words in the poem are a little awkward to pronounce, we want to avoid them for now and learn the melody without any unnecessary tensions.

Now, at last, you are ready for (Step 7): *combine the melody with the words.* If you have any problems putting words and music together, you can repeat some of the steps already done and work things out by yourself. Let's review the steps by listing them:

1. Write out the text in stanza form.
2. Paraphrase the poem and summarize its meaning.

3. Read the poem aloud with expression, phrasing, and accentuation.
4. Speak the poem in rhythm, breathing at the right times.
5. Learn the melody by ear.
6. Vocalize the melody until you can sing it smoothly.
7. Combine the melody with the words.

With these steps completed, memorization will come easily; then you can give all of your attention to expression. Chapter 9, "Performing a song," will tell you more about sharing your song with an audience.

Exercises

Although this chapter was not about vocal technique, it suggests some exercises to improve the musical quality of our singing. We will work on ear-training, phrasing, and dynamics.

5.1 *Do-Re-Mi Scale.* We all know these syllables from Rodgers and Hammerstein's song "Do-Re-Mi" in *The Sound of Music*. Sing either the English pronunciation:

do, re, mi, fa, so, la, ti, do

or the slightly different Italian version:

do, rɛ, mi, fa, sɔ, la, si, dɔ

as your teacher prefers. Purpose: to sing long tones with close attention to intonation.

5.2 *2-Note Sighs.* Connect these pairs of tones smoothly. Purposes: to practice the so-fa syllables, clear intonation, and catch breaths.

Do you sense that the pitches do and ti are closer to each other than the pitches ti-la, la-so, and so-fa? Also that fa and mi are closer to each other than mi-re and re-do? This may not be immediately clear, but with practice you will realize that do-ti and fa-mi are half-steps and the others are whole steps. Recognizing the half-steps helps us to sing accurately in tune.

5.3 *3-Note Sighs.* Connect these groups of tones smoothly. Purposes: the same as in exercise 5.2.

5.4 *Swell.* In order to sing expressively you have to be able to sing louder and softer. Begin with just three clear levels, soft (p), medium (mf), and loud(f). avoid "super-soft" and "super-loud" for now. Use consonants to help you make the gradations. Purpose: to realize that different volume levels are available throughout the voice.

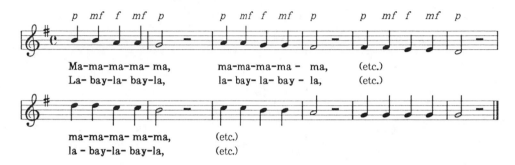

Ma-ma-ma-ma- ma,   ma-ma-ma-ma - ma,   (etc.)
La- bay-la- bay-la,   la- bay- la- bay - la,   (etc.)

ma-ma-ma- ma-ma,   (etc.)
la - bay-la- bay-la,   (etc.)

5.5 *Lover and Lass.* This phrase from the song by Morley (page 122) gives us a lively exercise for catch breaths. Purpose: to take catch breaths quickly and easily, without breaking the rhythm.

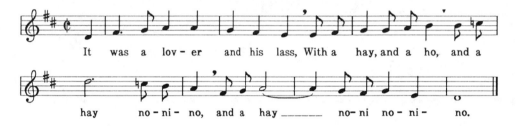

It was a lov - er and his lass, With a hay, and a ho, and a

hay no - ni - no, and a hay _____ no- ni no - ni - no.

Additional reading   *If you have just begun to enjoy poetry and want to know more about it, you would enjoy a short book by a fine American poet:*
Introduction to Poetry: Commentaries on Thirty Poems by Mark Van Doren. Hill and Wang, 1951.

6 Vowels and Vocal Color

Guiding questions: *Do I need to pay attention to words when I sing? Are vowels the same in singing as in speaking? How many vowels are there, and are there written symbols for them? How can I sing so that all vowels are equally easy and strong, so that I always use a good tone quality and still have variety?*

HAVE you ever heard someone speaking a language you do not understand? Did you enjoy it or were you bored? It may be fun to hear a few sentences in an unfamiliar language, but we usually grow bored with sounds that we can't understand.

Have you ever heard a singer whom you couldn't understand? The experience is much the same. We strain to catch what information we can; but if it is too difficult, we give up and settle into boredom. We are disappointed because we miss a large part of the pleasure that we should get from the song.

What a pleasure it is to hear a singer who has a beautiful tone, strong musical expression, and clear words—all at the same time! Because you want to become such a singer, you need to know the pitfalls that keep others from achieving success.

First, some singers simply don't realize that others are not understanding every word they sing. A good test is to practice with a sympathetic but honest listener who does not know your song and who will tell you if you are not making everything clear. Your teacher and your fellow voice students will probably be your most cooperative listeners. This kind of work takes time!

Second, many people have not learned to pronounce the English language distinctly and beautifully. Most of us have some regional speech habits that are distracting or unclear to people who come from other areas; and we find to our surprise that we habitually use pronunciations that others consider wrong. We need to learn standard American pronunciation, which sounds correct and appropriate to any English-speaking person in the United States or Canada.

Your speaking voice, singing, and diction

Singing is, first of all, saying. This maxim contains one of the keys to moving the emotions of an audience. Your listeners can't be persuaded if they don't know what you want to say.

It must be admitted that singing clearly is more difficult than speaking clearly. Music inevitably alters language sounds, by:

- stretching short vowels over long notes;
- giving full length and tone to syllables that might be very weak, or even omitted, in conversational speech;

- carrying the voice higher than it goes in normal speech. (Certain vowels become indistinguishable from each other on the higher notes of the female voice.)

Such problems can be overcome with knowledge, awareness, and thoughtful practice.

If your speaking voice is free and resonant, it furnishes the very best foundation and model for singing. We often use the rule *sing as you speak* to achieve spontaneity and strong projection.

The other side of the coin is that if your speaking voice is not free and resonant—if it is timid, breathy, or dull, or if you have an unpleasant regional twang or drawl—then your singing will suffer, too. Be open to the possibility that your speaking voice needs work in order to release the full potential of your singing voice.

The thought of changing your voice might please you—change is what education is all about! On the other hand, it may frighten you to change something that seems so intimately associated with your personal identity. Will people think you are putting on airs?

Actually, no one will ask you to change your everyday speaking voice unless you want to or unless your speech habits are unhealthful. You don't have to give up your familiar way of speaking when you learn new techniques for singing. A living example of this was Madeleine Marshall, who coached the English diction of some of the world's finest singers but spoke a twanging Brooklyn dialect in daily conversation. In speech, she was bilingual, able to speak Brooklynese or highly polished Standard American at will.

As a singer, you may find that you need various styles of diction, comparable to styles of dress. If you are going to perform in blue jeans, then your hometown accent will sound fine. If the performance requires dressing up, then your diction should be "dressed up" also. If you are in formal wear and standing in front of a symphony orchestra or if you are performing in a Shakespearean play, then you will want your diction to match the style of the occasion and the needs of the performance.

Diction describes the whole area of vocal technique related to making words clear. It includes several concepts that are summed up in this sentence: "We *pronounce words, enunciate vowels and syllables, and articulate consonants.*" When we do all of these well, we have *good diction.*

The International Phonetic Alphabet (IPA)

In school we all learned five vowel letters: *a, e, i, o, u,* and sometimes *y.* As singers, we need to think in terms of *sounds* rather than alphabet letters, and in this book from now on the word "vowel" means vowel sound. English has far more than five vowel sounds. We will draw the extra symbols we need from the International Phonetic Alphabet (abbreviated IPA).

Phonetics is the scientific study of speech sounds. Scholars of phonetics need a system of written symbols with which they can take written notes about the sounds of any language. The International Phonetics Association invented the IPA for that purpose. Each IPA symbol stands for only one sound and never for any other. When you have learned IPA symbols in English, they will be very useful in studying other languages as well.

When you use the IPA to write the sounds of a word or a whole text, the process is called *transcribing.* IPA transcriptions contain symbols only for what can be heard. When you transcribe words into IPA, omit all silent letters and punctuation. Do not use capital letters, because in some cases small and capital letters are used to indicate different sounds.

When IPA symbols occur in a normal context, they are enclosed in square brackets, as in this sentence: "The sound [ju] is spelled one way in cute [kjut] and another way in pew [pju]." Square brackets can enclose a letter, a word, or a whole text. If a whole text has been transcribed into IPA, you don't need separate brackets for each letter or word: one pair does the job.

Actors, announcers, and speech teachers all rely on Kenyon and Knott's *A Pronouncing Dictionary of American English*, which gives all pronunciations in IPA. Pronunciations given in this book all follow Kenyon and Knott's standard. If you are used to some other pronunciations, just be aware that they are not Standard American and might cause confusion.

All of the IPA symbols used in this book are listed for reference in Appendix B, page 253.

What vowels have in common

All vowels are made with an *unrestricted flow of breath*, in contrast to consonants, which all interfere with breath flow in some way. To make the various vowels, the lips and tongue change the shape of the mouth and throat resonators, but they never stop or slow down the breath flow. The vocal cords may also influence vowels, but voice scientists are not sure about this because of the difficulty of precisely measuring the vocal cords while they are in motion.

All vowels can be described by their quality as *bright, neutral, or dark vowels*. These qualities are inherent in the vowels when they are correctly produced. For instance, a well-produced bright vowel is naturally that way; you don't have to exert yourself to make it bright.

In each category, all vowels can also be described as being *closed or open* to some degree, referring to the amount of space between the tongue and the roof of the mouth (palate). We usually drop the jaw somewhat lower for singing than for speech, but the lifting of the tongue also plays a role here.

All vowels *can resonate freely* and most good singers train themselves to have a uniform sensation of vibration for all vowels. This sensation is at odds with speech theory, which frequently refers to "front vowels," "mid-vowels," and "back vowels." Such terms refer to the part of the tongue that is active in shaping the mouth resonator; it has nothing to do with the vibratory sensations experienced by good singers. This book does not use the term "back vowel" because it might mislead a student into making a throaty tone.

All vowels can be produced with the *tip of the tongue lightly touching the lower teeth*. Most singers find this position helpful for vocal relaxation.

The five cardinal vowels

In singing English we recognize fifteen vowels, but singers have traditionally done most of their vocalizing on five of them. We call these the "cardinal" or "principal" vowels because they are so distinctive that we never mistake them or confuse them with each other. The other vowels can all be described in comparison with the cardinal vowels.

All fifteen vowels are listed for reference in Appendix B, and the following list matches the numbering of the vowels on that list.

The cardinal vowels are:

IPA Symbol:	English name:	Some possible spellings:
1. [i]	Ee	bee, sea, brief, machine
3. [e]	Pure Ay	chaotic, dictates
6. [a]	Bright Ah	aisle (British: ask, dance)
10. [o]	Pure Oh	hotel, obey
12. [u]	OO	true, who, moo, few, through

brighter _____ *darker*

ee ay ah oh oo

back _____ forward

We will consider the cardinal vowels separately, from the brightest to the darkest.

1. [i], *Ee*, is the brightest of all vowels and the one with the least space between the tongue and palate. While the tip of the tongue touches the lower teeth, the front of the tongue (the area just behind the tip) is lifted forward until it is close to the upper teeth and the gum ridge just behind them. In singing [i], the mouth space usually needs to be larger than in speaking, but the opening is still smaller than for any other vowel.

Do you "smile and say cheese"? In fact, you can "say cheese" perfectly well without smiling at all. In a happy song you might use a smiling [i] if it is relaxed and appropriate, but the smile is not a necessity. In a more somber song you may choose to soften the brightness of [i] by rounding your lips in the direction of [u]. Think of the words "peace" and "sleep," for which a bright, edgy sound is inappropriate.

For natural, acoustical reasons, most female singers experience difficulty singing [i] on high pitches. Most sopranos substitute [e] on high notes for the sake of greater comfort and stronger resonance with no loss of clarity.

3. [e], *Pure Ay*, is a bright vowel, and its degree of openness is about halfway between [i] and [a]. As with [i], the tip of the tongue stays down and the lips are either smiling or neutral. There is more about this vowel later.

6. [a], *Bright Ah*, is the most open of the cardinal vowels. It is the true "Italian ah." In order to discover it, say all of the bright vowels in order, opening them gradually: [i,e,a].

Standard American pronunciation does not use [a] by itself, although it is used by some British, as well as some Easterners and Southerners. In chapter 8 we will see how important [a] is in diphthongs.

Whenever [a] occurs in British pronunciation, Standard American uses [æ], as in "chaff, laugh, command, branch, nasty, mast." If you ever want to sound British, for *Pirates of Penzance* or *Camelot*, for instance, sing [a] instead of [æ] in such words.

10. [o], *Pure Oh*, is a dark vowel, and its degree of openness is about halfway between [a] and [u]. A safe, easy way to darken [o] is to round your lips by moving the corners in toward the center. Let your tongue relax and stay low. To keep the vowel pure, let your mouth position stay the same, no matter how long the [o] lasts. More about this vowel later.

12. [u], *Oo*, is the darkest of all vowels. A safe, easy way to darken [u] is to round the lips. Let your tongue relax, lie forward, and touch the lower teeth. Most singers find it easy to sing [u] softly because of its natural darkness, but for projection of a strong tone it may be necessary to open [u] somewhat toward [o].

Many Americans have a tense way of speaking [u] without rounding the lips; they get the necessary closure by tensing and lifting the back of the tongue instead. You will have a much more beautiful and more comfortable sound if you learn to sing [u] with rounded lips and relaxed tongue. Think of [u] as a "hollow" sound, with a lot of space in the mouth in spite of the narrow opening formed by rounded lips.

The five cardinal vowels are the only ones needed for singing in Spanish.

Pure Ay and Oh in English. From a singer's point of view, Ay and Oh are seldom pure vowels in English. If you say Ay very slowly and listen carefully, you will hear the beginning vowel sound [e] change at the end to a sound like [i]. If you say Oh the same way, you will hear [o] change to a sound like [u] at the end. (You will also feel movement in your mouth as the vowels change.) Such combinations of two vowels, called *diphthongs*, are discussed in chapter 8.

Do we always make diphthongs out of Ay and Oh? Nearly always, especially when we speak slowly or when the vowels are in strong, stressed syllables. However, we might pronounce Ay and Oh as pure [e] and [o] when we speak rapidly or when they are in weak, unstressed syllables, as in the spelling examples above. Our ears interpret Pure Ay and Pure Oh as exact equivalents to their diphthong forms.

If they are equivalent in meaning, why does it matter that Ay and Oh have two forms? First, because music often slows words down so much that every detail can be heard; if the vowel is too pure, it sounds like a foreign accent. On the other hand, you may soon want to sing in Italian, and you will have to use pure [e] and [o] consciously to avoid an American accent.

Two more Italian vowels

Because Italians were the first to invent opera and to export singing stars to other nations, classical vocal study has traditionally emphasized the Italian language. Some teachers recommend that their students sing in Italian first in order to avoid the problems caused by poor speech habits in English. For these reasons we highlight two more vowels that are needed for both Italian and English pronunciation:

IPA Symbol:	English name:	Some possible spellings:
4. [ɛ]	Open Eh	met, less, head, said
9. [ɔ]	Open O (or Aw)	ought, dawn, haul, wall

4. [ɛ], *Open Eh*, is bright but considerably more open than [e]. With the tongue tip touching the lower teeth, the front of the tongue is lifted, but only a little. We can smile on [ɛ] if we want to, or we can round the lips in the direction of [ɔ] to make the sound more gentle or somber. In school we learned that [ɛ] is a short vowel, but in singing it lasts as long as the music requires.

[ɛ] is an easy vowel for most singers if they accept the natural brightness of the sound. Some Southern dialects mistakenly use [I] in place of [ɛ], changing "pen" to "pin," "ken" to "kin."

9. [ɔ] *Open O*, is dark but considerably more open than [o]. An easy way to darken [ɔ] is to round your lips slightly. [ɔ] is an advantageous vowel for many voices; most male singers find it their best one for vocalizing.

Unfortunately, many Americans grow up in areas where [ɔ] is not used at all in daily speech. Say these pairs of words out loud: "hock" and "hawk"; "la" and "law"; "sod" and "sawed"; "cot" and "caught."

The second word in each pair contains [ɔ]. If the paired words sound identical to your ears, you are among those who lack [ɔ] in their speech. Practice saying "hawk," "law," "sawed," and "caught" with your lips rounded in order to get used to this new sound. Again, you don't have to change your daily speech unless you want to, but welcome this new vowel into your vocabulary for the sake of good singing.

To sing in Italian you need all seven vowels described so far: [i, e, ɛ, a, ɔ, o, u]. To sing church Latin you need these five: [i, ɛ, a, ɔ, u].

Eight English vowels

The remaining vowels are so characteristic of English that they are difficult for most foreigners. Because we learned most of them as "short" vowels in spoken English, we have to focus carefully on their exact quality when they are stretched long by music. We will vocalize on the ones we need and become comfortable with them.

IPA Symbol:	English name:	Some possible spellings:
2. [ɪ]	Short I	sing, rely, been, women, busy
5. [æ]	Short A	sang, mash, marry, cat, carry
7. [ɑ]	Dark Ah	father, far, wander, watch
8. [ɒ]	Short O	cot, sorry, hock, gone
11. [ʊ]	Short U	full, put, good, would, woman
13. [ʌ]	Uh	". . . but young love does flood . . ."
14. [ə]	Schwa	*a* cact*u*s, th*e* nation,
15. [ɜ]	Er	serve, earth, girl, worth, hurt

2. [ɪ], *short I*, is a bright vowel, just a little more open than [i], but very similar to it when well sung.

Many Americans speak [ɪ] with the tongue pulled back, especially before or after [l], as in "little" or "ill." When this happens, the beauty and special color of the [ɪ] are lost. Practice saying [ɪ] with the tongue touching the lower teeth, and then say "sill" with the same clear vowel quality.

5. [æ], *Short A*, is a bright, open vowel. Some people shy away from the brightness of [æ], but it can be beautiful if the mouth opens freely and the tongue lies forward and relaxed.

[æ] has a bad reputation because it is sometimes spoken with unnecessary tension and/or nasality. Singers and choir directors often try so hard to avoid this ugliness that they change [æ] to [ɑ], so that "a man's hand" becomes "a mahn's hahnd." This is not a good British accent; it is just unclear and affected.

Contrary to general belief, [æ] is used by even the most cultivated British and American speakers. Remember that Shakespeare wrote *Hamlet*, not *Hahmlet*. If [æ] was good enough for Shakespeare, we can use it, too.

7. [ɑ], *Dark Ah*, lies in the center of the vowel color range. It is the most open of all vowels, meaning that the tongue lies quite low in the mouth, with the jaw as open as is comfortable. Because it is so open, [ɑ] is the vowel of choice for most classical vocalizing, especially for female singers' high notes.

[ɑ] can take on various shades of color, depending on the mood of the song. Individual speakers may use a variety of colors for this vowel, depending on their regional origin and preference. In order to find the normal or "real" [ɑ], which is exactly in the center of the color range, alternate [ɑ] with brighter and darker vowels: sing [ɑ i ɑ i ɑ] and [ɑ u ɑ u ɑ].

8. [ɒ], *Short O*, is a vowel that is used by some careful speakers of Standard American. It is as open as [ɑ] and only slightly darker. When [ɒ] is lengthened even a little by music, it becomes impossible to distinguish it from [ɑ]. We will not attempt to vocalize on [ɒ]; we will sing [ɑ] instead.

11. [ʊ], *Short U*, is the second darkest vowel, after [u], and it is only slightly more open than [u]. Practice it as you do [u], with your tongue touching the lower teeth and a feeling of hollowness in your mouth. Unlike vowel 8 [ɒ], this vowel keeps its quality even when lengthened for singing.

13. [ʌ], *Uh*, or "Ugh" if you prefer, is a moderately open neutral vowel. It is the fundamental sound of the human voice when the mouth and pharynx are not intentionally adjusted. It is so easy for most people to sing that many singers habitually sing [ʌ] when they mean to sing [ɑ]. Many vocal exercises in this book use this vowel because it is so open and relaxed. Again, let the tongue relax forward to touch the lower teeth.

14. [ə], *Schwa*, is always short and always weak (unstressed). It is a neutral vowel, a little less open than [ʌ]. [ə] changes according to its neighbors: it is brighter in a happy mood or with bright vowels around it; it is darker in a somber mood or with dark vowels around it. It is more open if it occurs between open vowels, more closed between closed vowels.

When we lengthen [ə] for singing, it usually sounds most like vowel 13 [ʌ]. If we were asked to vocalize a phrase on a schwa, we would use [ʌ].

Despite its weakness, [ə] deserves special study because contrast between strong and weak syllables is characteristic of English. In some languages (French and Japanese, for instance) all syllables have equal strength, but not in English. A singer who ignores this fact and sings all syllables with equal strength sounds laborious and monotonous.

Schwas occur often. Slowly say this sentence aloud; every word contains a schwa: "The handsome captain salutes a treasured woman." As you can see, any vowel letter, *a, e, i, o,* or *u,* can be used in the spelling of a schwa.

The name "schwa" comes from a Hebrew alphabet sign, *shva,* which usually indicates a weak vowel just like ours. Sometimes it shows that there is no vowel where one might be expected. English also has words in which we see a vowel letter but leave it out in pronunciation, as well as words in which no vowel is written but one must be sung. Here are some examples transcribed into IPA to show how they must be sung.

	Said:	Should be sung:
cotton	[ktn]	[kɑtən]
bottom	[btm]	[bɑtəm]
little	[lɪtl]	[lɪtəl]
didn't	[dɪdnt]	[dɪdənt]

In chapter 8 you will learn more about [ə] and its role in a family of schwa-diphthongs.

15. [ɜ], *Er,* is also a neutral vowel, like vowels 13 and 14, but it is less open and somewhat darkened. When most people hear this sound, they are less aware of the vowel than of the *r* that is always part of its spelling.

[ɜ], like vowel 5 [æ,] has a bad reputation because so many people sing it with tension and an ugly tone. An angry dog says "Grr," and some people go almost that far with this vowel.

To find a beautiful form of [ɜ], use the advice that was given for other dark vowels. Let your lips round slightly. Let your tongue lie low and forward in your mouth, while the middle of the tongue rises a little. Above all, avoid bunching up the back of your tongue as many people do when saying [r].

We can vocalize on [ɜ] if we completely remove all trace of [r] quality from the vowel. Practice saying "earth" and "hers" with no [r] at all. When you enunciate this vowel with no consonant sound, it is practically identical with the French vowel in *jeune* and the German vowel in *koennte.* Once you have found it, [ɜ] is an easy, advantageous vowel for most voices to vocalize.

Summary of fifteen vowels

Vowels 1–6, [i, ɪ, e, ɛ, æ,a] are all bright vowels, which require the tongue to lift and move forward. Use either smiling or relaxed lips. If you want to darken these vowels for mood, think them clearly but round the lips slightly.

Vowels 8–12 [ɒ, ɔ, o, ʊ, u] are all dark vowels; let the tongue remain low and relaxed. Let the lips round and darken the vowels, without tongue tension. If you want to brighten these vowels for mood, think them clearly but allow a little smile to widen the lip position.

Vowels 7 and 13–15 [ɑ, ʌ, ə, ɜ] are all neutral vowels that allow great variety of coloration according to mood. They can be made darker with lip-rounding or brighter with smiling, while still remaining understandable.

There are three vowels we do not vocalize:

- [a] always changes into either [æ] or [ɑ];
- [ɒ] changes to [ɑ] when sustained;
- [ə] changes to [ʌ] when sustained.

We will put off vocalizing vowels 3 and 10, [e, o], until we study them as diphthongs in chapter 8.

Equalizing the vowels

Almost everyone finds some vowels easier and stronger than others; our goal in exercising is to sing all vowels with equal comfort and equally strong resonance while we also give each vowel its own special sound. Because it is the most basic sound of the voice, we often use vowel 13 [ʌ] for a comparison with other vowels and adjust their resonance to be like it.

For the sake of evenness in singing, let your mouth open moderately for all vowels. Open vowels are likely to be naturally louder than closed vowels. Avoid over-opening the naturally open vowels [æ, ɑ]. Open up the closed vowels [i, ɪ, u, ʊ] much more than would seem right for their pure quality. Let [ʌ] be your model.

Also for the sake of evenness, avoid exaggerated mouth positions, such as grinning. Once you are sure that you understand what the various vowels are, form them as easily as possible.

Exercises

The following exercises use ten different vowel sounds for the reasons summarized earlier. You used cardinal vowels in earlier exercises; now we add five more vowels. Our basic exercise method is to sound vowels next to each other in groups of two or three. Compare and contrast them for yourself, and check your observations with your teacher and your fellow students.

From this point onward, all vocal exercises will use IPA symbols, except when whole English words are used. The IPA consonant symbols used here are pronounced with normal English sounds.

6.1   *Bright Vowels.* Sing smoothly, with clear vowel qualities and even dynamics. These vowels are in the words "me, muss, miss, mess, mat." Purpose: to establish the bright vowels and to compare each one with [ʌ].

mi   mʌ   mi   mi   mʌ   mi   mi   mʌ   mi   mi   mʌ   mi
mɪ   mʌ   mɪ   mɪ   mʌ   mɪ   mɪ   mʌ   mɪ   mɪ   mʌ   mɪ
mɛ   mʌ   mɛ   mɛ   mʌ   mɛ   mɛ   mʌ   mɛ   mɛ   mʌ   mɛ
mæ   mʌ   mæ   mæ   mʌ   mæ   mæ   mʌ   mæ   mæ   mʌ   mæ

6.2   *Dark Vowels.* Sing smoothly, just as in the last exercise. These vowels are in the words "do, good, law." Purpose: to establish the dark vowels and to compare each one with [ʌ].

du   dʌ   du   du   dʌ   du   du   dʌ   du   du   dʌ   du
gʊ   gʌ   gʊ   gʊ   gʌ   gʊ   gʊ   gʌ   gʊ   gʊ   gʌ   gʊ
lɔ   lʌ   lɔ   lɔ   lʌ   lɔ   lɔ   lʌ   lɔ   lɔ   lʌ   lɔ

6.3 *Nonsense waltz.* Sing smoothly. For fun, put emotions into these nonsense words, singing as if you were angry, jealous, giddy, etc. Purpose: to establish *legato* singing in vowels that English and Italian have in common.

Ah	heart,	calm	swans	bob	far. _____
Then	let	Peg's	friend	end	well. _____
"Feed	these	three	geese,"	she	pleads. _____
All	call,	"Ought	Paul	draw	naught?" _____
Do	you	woo	too	few	true? _____

Ah	heart,	calm	swans	bob	far. _____
Then	let	Peg's	friend	end	well. _____
"Feed	these	three	geese,"	she	pleads. _____
All	call,	"Ought	Paul	draw	naught?" _____
Do	you	woo	too	few	true? _____

6.4 *Tri-puh-lets.* Avoid any sound of consonant *r* in the second syllable. Purpose: to establish [3] as a singable vowel with no consonant character.

ma	m3	ma	ma	m3	ma
si	s3	si	si	s3	si
bu	b3	bu	bu	b3	bu

6.5 *Vowel Cousins.* The following pairs of vowels have the same degree of opening. They help to "tune" each other; in other words, improvement in one vowel will also lead to improvement in the other vowel paired with it.

i	u	i	u	i	u	i	u	i	u	i	u
I	U	I	U	I	U	I	U	I	U	I	U
ɛ	ɔ	ɛ	ɔ	ɛ	ɔ	ɛ	ɔ	ɛ	ɔ	ɛ	ɔ
æ	ʌ	æ	ʌ	æ	ʌ	æ	ʌ	æ	ʌ	æ	ʌ

Additional reading

For clear, humorous, and thorough instruction about singing words clearly:
The Singer's Manual of English Diction by Madeleine Marshall. Schirmerbooks, New York, 1953.

Singers, actors and broadcasters rely on:
A Pronouncing Dictionary of American English by John S. Kenyon and Thomas A. Knott. G. & C. Merriam Co., Springfield, MA, 1953.

7 Consonants and Clarity

Guiding questions: *How important are consonants? When I sing, will consonants help or get in the way? What if several consonants come together? Will they make my singing sound choppy?*

COMMON courtesy tells us to make it easy and pleasant for others to understand us. That's why we neither mumble nor shout at other people; we speak as clearly as we need to without overdoing. We will try to sing just that clearly, with the difference that we may want to sing in a large room for many people.

Some voice students become so concerned about energizing their vocal tone that they simply forget to energize their consonants. If your singing tone suddenly becomes strong enough to be heard 100 feet away, then the consonants also need to be strong enough to carry across the same distance. Some consonants carry almost as well as vowel tones, but others are weak sounds that must be exaggerated in order to be heard.

Aside from clear diction, some consonants actually help us to improve tone and clarify vowel quality. For that reason, we have already done a number of exercises that included consonant sounds.

Most IPA symbols for consonants are the same as normal alphabet letters. When you have learned the few new ones that are needed, you will be able to write whole words in IPA.

Semivowels, semi-consonants

We have two sounds in English that have vowel quality ("made with an unrestricted flow of breath," as we said in the last chapter) but cannot stand alone as vowels. They act like consonants in that they serve to start syllables. Because of their mixed characteristics, we call them semivowels or semi-consonants (the terms are interchangeable). They are also called "glides" because they involve changing rather than constant vowel sounds.

IPA Symbol:	English name:	Some possible spellings:
16. [j]	Yah	you, yes, unit, few, Europe
17. [w]	Wah	water, weed, wail, whoa!, one

16. [j], *Yah*, begins from an [i] position, with the tongue lifted forward. Say "you" in slow motion, slowly enough to hear the sound of [i] as you begin and the change that occurs as your tongue moves from [i] to [u], the main vowel of "you." If you sing "you" slowly, notice that the [i] sound must start on pitch. If you slide up to the pitch after you have already started singing, it sounds lazy and careless.

Notice that *u* and *ew* sometimes have the sound of [ju], even though no letter is present to represent the [j]. There also is a large group of words in which [j] is optional for everyday speech, but required for "dress-up" speech. (Do you remember the distinction we made between "blue jeans" singing and "formal" singing?). Practice these words, which may sound peculiar to you but which are required for formal singing.

Spelling:	IPA:	Examples:
du, dew	[dju]	due, dew, endure, duke
lu	[lju]	lute, allure (but not if a consonant precedes "l," as in "flute" or "blue")
nu, new	[nju]	new, news, nude, inure
su, sew	[sju]	suit, sewer, sue (but not "Susan")
	[zju]	resume
tu	[tju]	tune, Tuesday, student, stupid
th	[θju]	enthusiasm

17. [w], *Wah*, begins from a [u] position, with rounded lips. Say "we" in slow motion, slowly enough to hear the sound of [u] as you begin and the change that occurs as your tongue moves from [u] to [i], the main vowel. If you sing "we" slowly, notice that the [u] sound must start on pitch; otherwise, it sounds lazy and careless, as would the [j].

Consonants

What all consonants have in common is that they all interfere with our breath flow in various ways and to various degrees. The interference can occur at various places:

- at the lips;
- between the lower lip and the upper teeth;
- between the tongue and the teeth;
- between the tongue and the ridge behind the teeth (called the gum ridge);
- between the tongue and the hard palate.

There are technical terms to describe these locations and other characteristics of consonant sounds, but it is not necessary to memorize them. We only need to know some large categories used to describe consonants and then to consider each one individually.

The most important thing to notice about any consonant sound is whether it is *voiced or unvoiced,* that means whether or not the vocal cords vibrate during the sound. If the vocal cords are vibrating, then the consonant has a musical pitch. If the vocal cords are not vibrating, then the consonant is a noise that has no definite musical pitch.

How do you test whether the vocal cords are vibrating during a consonant? Just use a finger to stop one ear while you say the consonant, sustaining it, if possible. An easy one to test is [s]; stopping your ear makes no difference in its sound because it is merely a noise made at the front of the mouth. Contrast it with [z]; stopping your ear now makes you aware of the pitch that is coming up from the vocal cords.

Check every consonant as you read about it, and decide whether it is voiced or unvoiced. Voiced consonants, just like vowels and semi-consonants, must be kept on pitch and not allowed to slide up from below.

Hums

We have three "hums." Technically, they are called "nasal continuants" because breath moves only through the nose rather than the mouth and because we can continue them as long as breath lasts.

IPA Symbol:	English name:	Some possible spellings:
18. [m]	Em	ma, summer, rim
19. [n]	En	now, inner, ban
20. [ŋ]	Ing	singer, finger, angry, anchor

Every consonant involves some interference with the breath flow. Test all three hums to find out where the interference takes place. Which one stops the breath at the lips? At the gum ridge? Farther back on the palate? Are the hums voiced or unvoiced?

Use "clean attack" and "clean release" for hums just as you do for vowels. That means no glottal stops, no sliding up to pitch, no extra vowel at the end of the hum. Hums are so much like vowels that some teachers think it is a good idea to make them last at least twice as long in singing as they do in speech.

Hums help us to discover nasal resonance, to establish a habit of keeping the nasal passage open, and to warm up the voice quietly. Test all three hums softly in all parts of your voice for comfort and ease. Test how smoothly and evenly your breath flows by humming a melody softly, with a finger stopping one of your ears.

At the end of a word, many Westerners confuse Ing with En. Practice words like "singing" to be sure that they rhyme with "king" and not with "queen."

Oral consonants (not in pairs)

Most consonants naturally occur in pairs, one voiced and one unvoiced consonant produced in a similar way; but first we will learn four consonants that do not fit that pattern.

IPA Symbol:	English name:	Some possible spellings:
21. [l]	El	la, follow, sill
22. [r]	Ahr	rib, arrow, far
23. [h]	Aitch	hum, aha!
24. [hw]	Which	what whale?

21. [l], *El*, is made with the pointed tip of the tongue lightly and quickly touching the gum ridge. Centuries ago, Italians found [l] so easy to do that they made up the syllables "fa-la-la," which we still sing in old English songs.

Many English speakers say [l] with the tongue curled back along the hard palate, and this darkens the vowels that come before and after the [l]. Practice "lee-lee-lee" to brighten an [l] that is too dark.

In a word with a final [l], as in "call" or "steal," the vowel may be spoiled by the tongue rising gradually and too early toward the [l] position. Keep the vowel pure; be sure the final [l] is quick, light, and as late as possible.

22. [r], *Ahr*, causes more problems than any other consonant. The worst problem is the one just described for [l]: when [r] follows a long vowel, it may cause the tongue to rise gradually and thereby spoil that vowel by cutting short its sustaining potential. This is such a common fault that almost every voice student has to work on it.

The complete IPA has ten different symbols for *R* sounds heard in various languages, but for our purposes we need only three. We will try to simplify the bewildering number of ways in which people use Ahr.

a. [r], *American R,* is the one we normally use before a vowel or between two vowels. Excessive tongue tension may produce a harsh, nasal [r]; but if the tongue remains relaxed, there is no problem.

b. [ɚ] is an example of a schwa symbol with a tag added to indicate a *Final R* quality at the end of the vowel. We use this tag to indicate that an Ahr sound is faintly present, without letting it color the whole vowel. More about this in the next chapter.

c. *Dropped R* has no IPA symbol because it is not heard. In formal or British speech you may avoid the problem of a tense, nasal *r* by simply omitting it:

- before another consonant, as in "Carl, hard, north," pronounced "kahl, hahd, nawth"; or
- before a pause, meaning the end of a single word or any interruption in a sentence.

If you practice dropping final *r*, you will enjoy the tongue relaxation that results. You need, however, to put some final *r* quality back into your singing because most Americans find it a little distracting to hear no final *r* at all.

d. [ɾ], *Flipped R,* is used between vowels in British or "formal" diction. To discover this sound, say "veddy meddy" several times quickly, lightening the *dd* until the words "very merry" become clear. This book uses the [ɾ] only in Italian and Spanish texts, where *r* between two vowels is flipped.

e. [r], *Rolled R,* needs no special symbol in this book because it plays no role in English diction; it sounds foreign and affected in English. Rolled R is normal in all other languages used in this book, so [r] means Rolled R in foreign song texts. It is always rolled with the tip of the tongue, never the uvula. (Even in France, the so-called "Parisian," uvular *r* is used only in pop music.)

In summary, for English diction you need three kinds of *r:* American, Final, and Flipped. For other European languages you need two kinds of *r:* Rolled and Flipped.

23. [h], *Aitch,* is a noise of simple friction as air passes through the mouth. Usually, the noise comes from near the back of the mouth, but we can learn to make it high and forward in the mouth for the benefit of good tone. [h] is a typically quiet consonant which only projects in a large room if it is made vigorously.

24. [hw], *Which,* is an air friction noise produced by blowing through lips shaped for a [u]. We do not hear the [u] because the lips move quickly to the position of the following vowel. The double symbol, [hw], shows that the sound is frictional, like [h], and also involves a quick glide, like [w].

Oral consonants in pairs

The remaining sounds all occur in pairs: the unvoiced consonant, a noise produced by interfering with the breath flow; and the voiced consonant made with the addition of vocal cord vibration. Numbers 25–32 are "continuants," which can be kept going as long as breath lasts. Numbers 33–40 are all "stops", which completely stop the flow of air so that we hear the effect of the breath being stopped or released or both.

IPA Symbol:	English name:	Some possible spellings:
25. [f]	Eff	fa, often, phrase, laugh
26. [v]	Vee	vigor, over, verve
27. [θ]	Theta	thin, Cathy, path
28. [ð]	Edh	this, either, without, smooth
29. [s]	Ess	solo, essence, kiss, science
30. [z]	Zee	zoo, hazard, present, has
31. [ʃ]	Shah	show, social, nation, sure
32. [ʒ]	Zsa-Zsa	azure, pleasure, massage
33. [p]	Pee	peach, upper, cup
34. [b]	Bee	beach, baby, cub
35. [t]	Tee	teach, atom, cut
36. [d]	Dee	do, odor, head
37. [k]	Kay	keep, tack, calm, accurate
38. [g]	Hard Gee	go, again, tag
39. [tʃ]	Cha-Cha	church, achieve
40. [dʒ]	Soft Gee	gem, jelly, ridge, rajah

Cononants 25–40 are all familiar to any English-speaking person and seldom cause difficulties. If you have trouble with a lisp or a "lateral s," you should work with a speech specialist.

Consonants vary in carrying power from [s], which can be clearly heard even in the softest whisper, to [p], the weakest of all consonants. For public speaking or singing, unvoiced consonants often need an extra burst of air, called an *aspiration*. This is what conductors mean when they say "Spit out your consonants!" Unfortunately, choral singers often respond to that command by using more facial tension instead of using more breath.

A special word about the six stops, 33–38: a stop at the end of a word may not be understood unless we add an extra sound. For instance, if you end a word like "sip" with your mouth closed, the final consonant will probably not be heard; the word could just as well be "sit" or "sick."

For an unvoiced final [p], [t], or [k], add aspiration. Practice "sap, sat, sack" with a small burst of air after each final consonant.

The voiced finals [b], [d], and [g] all need a weak schwa for carrying power on the release. Practice singing "rib, rid, rig" with a weak vowel after each final consonant—on pitch, of course!

Keeping in mind the special case of final [b], [d], and [g], here is one more reminder: Voiced consonants must have the same clean attack and clean release that you give to vowels. That means that they start on pitch without a glottal attack and they end on pitch with no extra sound afterward.

Clusters and legato singing

Our language is rich in consonants. Think of an ordinary sentence like "This plant sprouts from seeds," which has five vowels and seventeen consonant sounds. Between the vowel in "plant" and the vowel in "sprouts" there are five consecutive consonants, three of which are unvoiced. No wonder it is difficult to sing smoothly in English!

Some singers become so intent on singing smoothly—the Italian word is *legato*—that they leave out consonants altogether or they articulate them weakly and flood them out with a stream of vowels. Such singing leaves no gap in the sound but unfortunate gaps in the meaning of the words. Listeners catch a bit of a word here and there and struggle to hear what the song is about. They are likely to go home saying, "I don't like to hear singers much. You can never understand them." We do not want that to happen!

No book can give separate exercises for all of the thousands of combinations of two, three, four, and five consonants that occur in English. We can, however, work for clarity and agility with tongue twisters and rapid speech patterns.

There are two excellent ways to develop good diction in the songs you work on: whispering and chanting.

If your consonants are too weak, try whispering the words of your song loudly enough so that your whisper can be heard across the room. You will immediately sense the energy level that vigorous articulation requires, and then you can use this level in your singing. Loud whispering is fairly strenuous; do it only for short periods of time.

If your diction is choppy, try chanting the text of a song on a single pitch. At first, let the timing be free so that you can concentrate solely on the clarity of the vowels and consonants. Pay special attention to the way one word connects to another. Let the final consonant of one word connect with the beginning of the next word, unless your ear tells you that the words have to be separated to make sense. When your chanting is smooth, try doing it in the correct rhythm of the song. Let the legato you have developed carry over into your singing.

Speaking exercises

Speak these words in a galloping singsong rhythm, quickly and lightly. Let the speed increase until you can speak all four lines in one breath. Purpose: to sensitize the main articulators and develop agility.

> The lips, the teeth, the tip of the tongue,
> the lips, the teeth, the tip of the tongue,
> the lips, the teeth, the tip of the tongue,
> the tip of the, tip of the, tip of the tongue!

Tongue twisters and many poems make excellent articulation drills. Learn to speak the following rapidly and clearly, and then sing them on comfortable middle to low pitches.

> A tutor who tooted a flute
> Once tutored two tooters to toot.
>   Said the two to the tutor
>   "Is it harder to toot,
> Or to tutor two tooters to toot?"

> Peter Piper picked a peck of pickled peppers. A peck of pickled peppers Peter Piper picked. If Peter Piper picked a peck of pickled peppers, where's the peck of pickled peppers Peter Piper picked?

> Blow, bugle, blow, set the wild echoes flying,
> Blow, bugle; answer, echoes, dying, dying, dying.
>   —Alfred Lord Tennyson, from "The Princess"

> Boot, saddle, to horse, and away!
> Rescue my castle before the hot day
> Brightens to blue from its silvery gray.
> Boot, saddle, to horse, and away!
>   —Robert Browning, from "Boot and Saddle"

Because of its meaning, the following poem must be spoken slowly but with perfectly precise articulation.

> I stepped from plank to plank
>   A slow and cautious way;
> The stars about my head I felt,
>   About my feet the sea.
>
> I knew not but the next
>   Would be my final inch,
> This gave me that precarious gait
>   Some call experience.
>   —Emily Dickinson

Singing exercises

7.1 *La-Beh-Da.* Sing these syllables one measure at a time until you are used to them, then let the speed increase until you can sing all three measures in one breath. (These syllables alternate lip and tongue consonants. They have been used by singers since the 1700s.) Purpose: to develop articulatory agility on a musical pattern.

[la- be- da- mε- ni- pɔ- tu- la-   bε- da- mε- ni- pɔ- tu- la- bε-

da- mε- ni- pɔ- tu- la- bε- da- mε]

7.2 *Connections.* Use these words to test yourself on some of the common problems mentioned in the chapter. Purpose: to exercise consonant connections and consonants that are often misused.

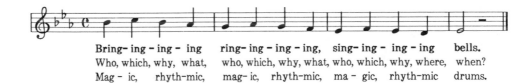

Bring- ing – ing – ing   ring- ing – ing – ing,   sing- ing – ing – ing   bells.
Who, which, why, what,   who, which, why, what, who, which, why, where,   when?
Mag - ic,   rhyth-mic,   mag- ic,   rhyth-mic,   ma - gic,   rhyth-mic   drums.

7.3 *Yah-Yah.* Sing this pattern with many different consonants and vowels. Be sure that voiced consonants begin on pitch and that the lowest note is in tune. This works well with a teacher or student leading and the class echoing back. Purpose: to assure that all vowels, semivowels, and voiced and unvoiced consonants can be sung both high and low in the voice.

ja	ja	ja	ja		ja	ja	ja	ja
wi	wi	wi	wi		wi	wi	wi	wi
zo	zo	zo	zo		zo	zo	zo	zo
blu	blu	blu	blu		blu	blu	blu	blu, etc.

Additional reading

In addition to the books by Madeleine Marshall and by Kenyon and Knott, there is a wealth of tips and practice materials in:
The Busy Speaker's Pocket Practice Book by Belle Cumming Kennedy and Patricia Challgren. Samuel French, Inc., New York and Hollywood, 1970.

8 Double and Triple Vowels

Guiding questions: *How does one sing syllables with more than one vowel? What about final r?*

IF you were a foreigner trying to learn English, what would you think of English spelling and pronunciation? Our letters do not always stand for the same sound, and most of our vowels lie somewhere in between the cardinal vowels. Beyond all that, some of our most common sounds are not single vowels at all but combinations of two or three vowels that are heard and understood as single sounds.

In chapter 6 we noticed that Ay and Oh, when they are spoken slowly, consist of combinations of vowel sounds. Such combinations are called *diphthongs* and *triphthongs*, Greek words that mean "double sounds" and "triple sounds." (Pronounce the "ph" carefully as [f] in both "dif-thong" and "trif-thong".)

Probably every language has compound vowel sounds, but most languages spell them out clearly with one letter for each vowel. English spelling sneaks diphthongs in without showing them: the phrase "I go" appears to have two vowels in it, but actually it has two diphthongs, adding up to four vowels. Some people become frustrated with such problems and say that the English language has no pure vowels, but that is not true either.

As singers, we know that our words will be prolonged by music and that every detail of our pronunciation will be noticeable to our audience. How will we sing "I go" if the music makes each syllable last for several seconds?

Five diphthongs

All English diphthongs follow this pattern: *the first vowel is stronger and more open, and the second vowel is weaker and more closed.* (If the weaker vowel comes first, we call it a semivowel or semi-consonant, as in the syllables [ju] or [wa].)

The strong-vowel-weak-vowel pattern leads to a simple but important rule for singing diphthongs: *stay on the stronger vowel as long as possible and sing the weaker vowel as late and as quickly as possible.* Some speech teachers use the term "vanish vowel" to describe the weak vowel of a diphthong.

The key to singing diphthongs well is knowing exactly what vowel sounds you wish to sing. The spelling does not always help. Some of us speak local dialects that close the vowels more than necessary; our singing will be more comfortable and pleasant with correct Standard American diphthongs.

These are the five main diphthongs. Each one can be identified by the numbers of the two vowels that make it up.

IPA symbol:	English name:	Some possible spellings:
4+2. [ɛɪ]	Long Ay	late, may, raise, weigh
6+2. [aɪ]	Long I	I, pie, my, aisle
9+2. [ɔɪ]	Ow	how, house
6+11. [aU]	Ow	how, house
10+11. [oU]	Long Oh	so, low, moan

4+2. [ɛɪ], *Long Ay*, was described in chapter 6 as a combination of vowels 3+1, [ei], in speech. In singing, this combination turns out to be too tense for comfort, and it is often misunderstood as [i]. The sound is better and clearer if we use 4+2, [ɛɪ], prolonging [ɛ] as the main vowel. In order to relax this sound and clarify it in your mind practice "late," as leh-eh-eh-it or [lɛ ɛ ɛ ɪt]; "may," as meh-eh-eh-ih or [mɛ ɛ ɛ ɪ]; "raise," as reh-eh-eh-ihz or [r ɛ ɛ ɛ ɪz].

This pronunciation may seem peculiar when you say it, but it will be just right when you sing it.

6+2. [aɪ], *Long I*, consists of Bright Ah and Short I in Standard American, producing a clear but relaxed pronunciation. If you want to make a country-western sound, try changing the second vowel to [i] and spend extra time on it.

9+2. [ɔɪ], *Oy*, uses Open Oh and Short I. Even if your local dialect does not use Open Oh alone, you probably use it in this diphthong.

6+11. [aU], *Ow*, consists of Bright Ah and Short U. Just as [i] is too closed for good singing of diphthongs, so is [u], and we use [U] instead for the vanish vowel.

10+11. [oU], *Long Oh*, consists of Pure Oh and Short U. Be sure that the first vowel is a clear Oh; some British dialects use a mixed vowel much like #15, [3], with no Oh quality at all.

Schwa-diphthongs

We learned in chapter 7 about problems caused by *r* if it is spoken with too much tension in the tongue. For relaxation practice, or for very formal English, you may want to drop *r* completely at the end of a syllable or at the end of a word. If you do so, you will discover some words in which you can say [ə] instead of [r].

Here is an example: "or." In daily speech most Americans say a vowel plus a consonant, [ɔr]. If you want to avoid American *r* and its tongue tension, you can say [ɔə] and, although it will sound formal, everyone will understand you. To sound less formal, you can put some [r]-coloring into the schwa, saying [ɔɚ]: the tag on the schwa shows that [r]-coloring is heard, but it does not completely cover up the vowel quality of the schwa.

There are four such diphthongs in which a schwa replaces a final *r* or *re*. All four can be spoken with [r]-coloring or without it. Because [r]-coloring is normal and correct in Standard American, we show it in IPA by adding a tag to the schwa.

Remember to relax your tongue when practicing schwa-diphthongs.

IPA Symbol:	English name:	Some possible spellings:
2+14. [ɪɚ]	Ear-Diphthong	beer, bier, mere, shear, we're
4+14. [ɛɚ]	Air-Diphthong	bear, care, there, their, e'er
9+14. [ɔɚ]	Or-Diphthong	shore, soar, your, door, o'er
11+14. [Uɚ]	Tour-Diphthong	cure, poor, your, you're

You can practice these diphthongs just as you do the five main diphthongs. Most important: make the first vowel sound clear, even though the spelling may look confusing. You can try out various amounts of [r]-coloring from none at all to a country twang.

Keep in mind that schwa-diphthongs occur only at times when *r* can be omitted, that is, before a consonant or before a silence (for instance, when you take a breath). If *r* comes before a vowel, the consonant [r] must be clearly pronounced, and there is no schwa-diphthong. Some examples:

- hear it [hɪrɪt]
- swear it [swɛrɪt]
- pour it [pɔrɪt]
- assure it [əʃurɪt]

- hereafter [hɪræftɚ]
- wherever [hwɛrɛvɚ]
- forever [fɔrɛvɚ]
- curable [kjʊrəbəl]

Schwa-triphthongs

Going one step further, we find that dropping a final *r* or *re* after a diphthong results in a triphthong. If you have worked through the above, you will have no trouble with these sounds.

IPA symbol:	English name:	Some possible spellings:
6+2+14. [aɪə]	Ire-Triphthong	fire, briar, lyre, choir
6+11+14. [aʊə]	Our-Triphthong	sour, flower

In both triphthongs [a] is prolonged in singing; the weaker vowels come quickly and lightly to end the tone. Again, if the next sound is a vowel, the *r* must be pronounced, and there is no schwa.

Our goal in learning about schwa-diphthongs and schwa-triphthongs was to reduce the amount of tongue tension associated with the consonant *r*. We often think of formality as stiffness; but in this case, formality in speech means relaxation and ease in the use of the tongue.

Exercises

8.1 *Diphthongs.* Practice this pattern with many different words that contain diphthongs. These words are written in IPA; what are they? Purpose: to identify the vowels that must be lengthened in the five main diphthongs.

[lɛ ɛ ɛ ɛ ɛ ___ ɪt	lɛ ɛ ɛ ɛ ɛ ___ ɪt]	Late.
[ma a a a a ___ ɪ	ma a a a a ___ ɪ]	My.
[dʒɔ ɔ ɔ ɔ ɔ ___ ɪ	dʒɔ ɔ ɔ ɔ ɔ ___ ɪ]	Joy.
[ha a a a a ___ ʊ	ha a a a a ___ ʊ]	How.
[so o o o o ___ ʊ	so o o o o ___ ʊ]	So?

8.2 *Diphthong and Triphthong Slurs.* Purpose: to identify the components of the schwa-diphthongs.

We're _____	there, _____	for _____	sure. _____
Mere _____	wear _____	for _____	poor. _____
Fire _____	our _____	choir _____	power. _____

9 Performing a Song

Guiding questions: *How can I get the most feeling out of a song—is there a "right way" or can I do it all my own way? What is "style"? How can I keep a song interesting from beginning to end? What is the role of my accompanist? How can I get over stage fright? How should I behave on stage and how can I get the meaning of a song across to an audience?*

FOR weeks or months now, you have been learning about the technique of singing: how your voice works, how to sing so that your voice sounds its best and does what you want it to do. There is much more to learn, but you can now sing songs, using what you have already learned.

Should you wait to sing songs until your voice is "perfect"? No. In fact, your vocal technique will develop more quickly if you combine working on technique and working on songs. Many singers only do their best when they are lifted up and carried along by the emotional energy of a song that they love. Also, your voice learns to function comfortably and reliably when you sing the same music many times, staying alert to your goals of beautiful tone and physical ease.

The goal of all of our work is to reach the point where we share our music with others. When that time comes, we trust that our good practice habits keep us singing well while we concentrate on the music that we want our listeners to enjoy with us.

Guidelines for interpretation

Notes printed on a page—we call them music, but there really is no music until we make the sounds that the printed notes stand for. When we go beyond merely making the sounds and communicate the message that was in the mind of the person who composed the music, then we can say that we are "interpreting" the music. Interpretation means that we go beyond the technical/mechanical step of making the right sounds and we move into the psychological and aesthetic areas of music.

In the process of learning a song (chapter 5) we learned that *the words come first.* Before a folksinger can make up a ballad there has to be a story to tell, and before a composer can write a song there has to be a good poem to inspire the music. It is the same for us as singers: before we can interpret a song well, we have to understand the words and feel good about putting them across to other people. After that, what we do with the music must always fit the words and never go against them.

Another principle that we all know from intuition and experience is that *rhythm is the heartbeat of music.* If the rhythm is weak or unsteady, the music can only be the same. Even though we know this, we sometimes become so concerned about tone quality and other aspects of music that we let the rhythm waver or stop altogether.

There are two rhythmic principles that will keep you from "losing the beat." First, *the rhythm starts with the first note of music and continues until the last note dies away*. If there is a piano introduction, start singing mentally with the first note you hear. If you have a rest during the song, sing through it mentally. If there is a postlude after the song, keep singing mentally until it dies away. If you neglect this rule and let your mind wander during the music, the people who are listening may not know exactly what went wrong, but their minds will wander too. What should you do during interludes when you are not singing? Simply listen to the piano. If you are sincerely enjoying the music, your enjoyment will show and the audience will pay attention too.

Second, *you may hurry or slow down any note of music at any time for any interpretive reason*. You have complete freedom—and complete responsibility. Tempos often quicken in order to express excitement. Even more often, tempos slow down in order to focus expression on a certain note or series of notes or to express some degree of relaxation or satisfaction or some other feeling. No rule tells us exactly when and how much to vary tempos; our imaginations must tell us.

Because music is an art, no one can say that a song must be performed in a certain way and no other way. The personal feelings that you bring to the music and the personal point of view that you have toward the words will be appreciated. On the other hand, we want to know that your way of doing a song is true to the composer's ideas. If this is not the case, we may ask why you chose to sing that song instead of some other song that fits your taste better. All of this brings us to the subject of musical styles.

Musical styles

The word "style" means many things in musical performance. Here are some examples of the ways in which musicians talk about it. Try to relate these to actual pieces of music and actual singers that you have heard.

1. Style can mean a type of music: "classical music" in contrast to "pop music," "ragtime" in contrast to "rock and roll."

2. As to historical period, music in the Classical style might contrast with Baroque music, which came before it, and Romantic music, which came after it.

3. As to expression, dramatic style uses more exaggerated emotional language than lyrical style.

4. As to specific composers or schools, we speak of ways of performing their music as being in their style or not in their style.

5. Your personal style belongs to you alone, and we recognize your singing by your style. Your individual vocal quality plays a role in your style, as well as your tendency to do certain things well, but your projection of your personality is also an important aspect of your style. When you develop your personal style, you learn to eliminate sounds that imitate other singers and replace them with sounds that are yours alone.

How do you learn about style? By listening thoughtfully to many kinds of music, done by many kinds of performers. Reading about music and musicians will help you build a vocabulary and define your ideas about styles. Through listening, reading, discussion, and experimentation you will learn what musical styles you like best, what styles you most want to perform, and how to develop a personal style.

Beginning, middle, and end

Because we cannot see music and because it goes by us in time, we often talk about it in words that describe shapes, using expressions like "the rise and fall of melody," "thin and thick textures," or "symmetrical form."

In general, we use the word "form" to describe patterns of repetition or non-repetition in music. One reason for learning about form is that music is easier to memorize if we understand its shape. An even more important reason is that awareness of musical form helps you to perform better. If we are aware of form ourselves, we can help the audience to know when a song repeats, where the climax is, and when the end is coming.

Many songs are written in *stanzas*, verses, using the same music two or more times to different words. We say that such songs are *strophic*, derived from the Greek word for "a turning," because a singer would usually turn from one side of the audience to the other at the end of a stanza (not a bad idea!). A good melody is worth hearing more than once, but the disadvantage of a strophic song is that the audience may lose interest or may not know when the song is over. You can help the audience by doing something special with the last stanza: a slight delay in starting it or a surge of extra energy or both; a slight change in tempo; holding out a particular note or stretching out a phrase for extra expression. Consider using these and other ways to provide a climax and to let the audience know that the story of the song is over.

Songs that are not strophic are said to be *through-composed*, meaning that the composer wrote new music for every part of the poem, although there can also be patterns of repetition. One pattern is so common that it is called "three-part song form": a stanza of music, a stanza of contrasting music, and then a repetition of the first stanza of music, with either the same words or new words.

Many popular songs and Broadway songs follow a "pop-song form" that is worth learning because it occurs so often. Two four-measure phrases make up an eight-measure melody, called "the 1st 8," which is repeated with new words as "the 2nd 8." For variety's sake, a different melody follows, also 8 measures long, called the "bridge" or "release." Then the first melody comes back in the "return." "Ain't Misbehavin' " is a good example of pop-song form.

- mm. 1–8   Introduction
- mm. 9–24   Verse (background reasons for the song)
- mm. 25–32 1st 8
- mm. 33–40 2nd 8
- mm. 41–48 Bridge
- mm. 49–56 Return

"A Cockeyed Optimist" also has pop-song form, but the main sections of the song are each sixteen measures long rather than eight. In order to build a strong climax, the return is stretched out an extra eight measures ("not this heart"); in pop music such an extra ending is called a "tag" or a *coda*. Which other songs in this book have pop-song form? Which have tags?

Whether you are singing Broadway or classical songs, you can help your audience enjoy your song more if you make the form clear in your performance. Here are some ways:

- Allow a little extra time, even a silence, between the verse and the chorus.
- Change your delivery in some way to call attention to the contrasting section or bridge; perhaps this is the time to move or change your posture.
- Slow down just a little at the end of the bridge so that the return brings back the first tempo along with the melody.

These are suggestions; not every one will work in every song. Whatever song you sing, decide where its climax is. Plan how you will build toward the climax and how you will relax the energy of the song afterward.

The accompanist

Every thinking singer knows that the piano accompanist is a Very Important Person. A good accompanist can make you sing better than you ever thought you could, and a poor one can make you sound as if you never practiced at all. A friendly accompanist makes it easier and more pleasant for you to perform, but a thoughtless accompanist can drown you out and completely distract the audience from what you want to do. It is worthwhile to find the best accompanist you can and to treat that person well.

Provide your accompanist with good sheet music to play from. I have seen someone walk into an audition, hand the pianist a folded, gray photocopy (illegal), and say, "I sing this down from where it's written." Such behavior shows ignorance and thoughtlessness. Remember that if the accompanist plays wrong notes because the music is illegible or if a flimsy page falls off the piano, it is your performance that suffers.

Give your accompanist enough time to learn the music. Choose your music and give it to the accompanist well ahead of the due date.

Some pianists are willing to transpose (play a song in a different key from the written one), and some are not; few pianists are willing to transpose at sight. Transposing is a complex mental skill that not every musician develops.

Take rehearsals seriously. Prepare your music and arrive on time, ready to work. Rehearsals help each of you to understand how best to help the other. *Let your pianist express opinions* both about the music and about your singing. You can learn a lot from an experienced pianist. If you are momentarily singing out of tune or have accidentally learned a wrong note, it is certainly better to let the pianist say so than to remain unaware of an error.

Later in this chapter there is more advice about how to relate to your accompanist onstage, but one more important matter belongs here: *Be sure your accompanist feels well paid,* whether in money or in appreciation or both.

Confidence and stage fright

By singing regularly for your voice teacher and other voice students you have gone a long way toward feeling comfortable about public performance. Even so, it is natural to feel some extra concern about doing your best in front of others. For some singers this natural desire to do well takes the exaggerated form of "stage fright," which hampers them and distracts from their real goal of communication. Almost everyone suffers from stage fright at some time in life, but we can learn to minimize it so that we enjoy the excitement of performing without the negative effects of fear.

Confidence lies in knowing that you can do well and that your listeners will like what you present to them. After all, you are gracious in recognizing the good in other singers' performances, and you should recognize the good in your own.

Some people judge themselves too harshly, often because they remember other persons in their past whom they tried unsuccessfully to please. It may be necessary to do some mental work to deal with those "internal judges." Here is one approach: Imagine your judges sitting in the audience while you perform, and picture smiles on their faces. (If those persons, in fact, cannot express any pleasant feelings, that is their problem.)

Should you not criticize yourself? Yes, in the practice room or in class, but *not at all on stage.* Learn to criticize yourself objectively. Objective self-criticism sounds like this: "I forgot some words in the second verse, and I think I sang flat in the last phrase." Objective self-criticism says that you want to improve and gives others a chance to help you by agreeing or disagreeing with your evaluation of your performance.

Subjective self-criticism, complaining, sounds like: "I was awful, and I blew the whole thing!" Such criticism gets in the way of improvement because it keeps you from thinking about specific ways to do better. This kind of evaluation becomes tiresome to other people because it is self-centered. It shuts the door to comments from others. (If you say you sang terribly, then anyone who says otherwise must be ignorant or insincere or both.) Learn to thank others for their positive comments and to invite their suggestions for improvement.

The essential ingredient to confidence is preparation. As part of your daily practice, think of preparing for a performance: Can you sing right after eating? How much warm-up do you need? How are you affected by what you did in the last 24 hours? Can you sing your song acceptably every day or only on rare occasions when you feel especially good?

If you can sing your songs well every day for a week before the performance, then you need have no fear about singing them on the performance day, too. If a song is not reliable for you on a daily basis, then keep it in the practice room and put a more comfortable song in front of the public. I have heard competitions in which one young singer after another tried feats that were not yet dependable; as a result they sang desperately and without musical expression. They would have done better by singing easier arias with confidence and feeling.

As a performance approaches, learn what you can about the audience for whom you will sing. Visit the place and practice on the stage where you will perform, if possible. Plan how you will enter and where you will stand. Plan what you will wear and be sure that the neckline and waistline feel comfortable when you breathe. Plan anything that you will need to say: Will you welcome the audience? Will you introduce yourself and your accompanist? Will you introduce your songs? Do you know how to pronounce the titles and composers of your songs? Being prepared is the key to confidence.

A special note to college students and to singers who enter competitions: you may be singing before a committee of voice teachers. Rather than being a tough, supercritical audience, voice teachers are the most sympathetic listeners you could have. They have heard many beginners, and they know the pitfalls of singing. Voice teachers are intensely interested in voices, otherwise they would not be in their profession, and they sincerely want you to succeed. Sing to them as you would to an audience of friends. Forgive them if their unpleasant duty of writing criticisms and giving grades sometimes causes them to forget their best selves.

Onstage

If you have done all of the preparations described above, the perfomance onstage is a natural climax to a pleasant process. One of the best mental attitudes to maintain is that the stage is your home, that the members of the audience are your guests at a party, and that the music is entertainment (even the food) that you are offering to them. This little game of the imagination takes your attention away from yourself and focuses it on making sure that your listeners have a good time.

The performance of classical music is a somewhat formal situation, but only because we want everyone to enjoy the music without any distraction or annoyance. Formality carried too far looks so stiff that no one enjoys the performance; informality carried too far looks disorganized and indifferent. Stage etiquette does not mean a list of rules that we "must" obey; it simply means a way of doing things smoothly and without fuss.

The singer enters the stage first, followed by the accompanist and the page-turner, if any. You both walk to your places at a normal rate. If possible, avoid crossing in front of someone else and avoid turning your back to the audience. If the audience welcomes you with applause, bow slightly to thank them. Simply lean forward enough to take a good look at your shoes; that is a bow.

If there is no printed program, you need to say hello to the audience and introduce yourself and your accompanist. Speak clearly, audibly, and slowly enough so that everyone can understand you. In addition to saying the name of your song and its composer, you may want to tell the audience something of interest about your song. People feel that they know you better if you talk, as well as sing, to them, and you may find that their positive acceptance of what you say puts you more at ease.

If your song is in a foreign language, be sure that you give a summary of what it is about, either orally or in the printed program. It is impolite to confront your guests with words they do not understand unless you explain what you are saying.

When you are ready to sing, be sure that the first words of the song are in your mind. Take a good breath and let it out again silently, making sure that your breathing muscles are not stiff. You may give a nod to the accompanist to begin the song or you may let the accompanist sense when you are ready; agree beforehand on a preference. From the first note of the introduction, you are already in the mood of the song.

In case your song has no piano introduction, agree with your pianist to play your starting note quietly as the top note of the first chord of the song. You may hum the note quietly if that helps you feel confident about starting correctly.

"Well begun is half done," says a wise proverb. Give full attention to the first notes you sing, making sure you give them enough time and enough energy to be heard clearly. Once the song is launched on its way, give your attention to the meaning of the words and what you want to say to the audience. Keep thinking ahead, so that when you end a phrase, the next phrase is already fully formed in your imagination.

"The eyes are the windows of the soul," says another proverb. Your listeners want more than just to hear your voice—they want you to communicate with them personally. In two or three minutes you can direct some of your song to every part of the audience. If you think that seeing faces may disturb you, try focusing on a point just between two persons' heads. Singing with your eyes either closed or raised to the ceiling is not a good practice; people quickly see that you are singing "over their heads" and their minds will tend to wander.

Keep the mood of the song through piano interludes, through all of your own singing (whether you are pleased with it or not), and through the ending of the song until the last note stops sounding.

May you use gestures? Yes, of course, keeping in mind what we said earlier about formality. Pointless arm-waving detracts from the music, but unnatural stiffness detracts as well. Let the music and the words tell you what to do; a gesture that flows naturally from the meaning of the song will enhance your performance.

What about mishaps? Stay in the mood of the song. Think ahead to the next phrase on which you and the pianist can get together and go on. Most mishaps go by without the audience knowing or caring; they still enjoy the song if you go on performing without giving off distress signals. If a singer is in trouble, it is not a good idea to flash a glance at the accompanist; the glance advertises the problem and looks like an attempt to put blame on the innocent pianist.

When the song ends, you can finally let go of your concentration, and that lets the audience know the song is over. Bow again modestly, just as you did before; a bow says, "Thank you for listening to me." After acknowledging the audience, smile at the accompanist, again to say, "Thank you." After a group of several songs or after a particularly difficult piece, gesture to your accompanist to stand and take a bow with you. Then you both leave the stage together, usually in the order in which you entered the stage.

Courtesy in performance means that you put the audience's pleasure ahead of your own. You do all that you can to make them comfortable. If you do not feel well, you decide (with your teacher) whether to sing or not to sing; but you do not worry the audience by making an apology about being sick. An apology makes people fear that you are hurting yourself, and maybe even your voice, on their account. Similarly, behave with courtesy at the end of a performance, even if you are disappointed with your own singing. Anyone who has enjoyed your singing deserves to receive your thanks, not your disgust over slight mishaps.

Additional reading

A rare old book, still found in many libraries, that gives hundreds of examples of good and bad interpretation, all discussed with logic and British wit:

Interpretation in Song by Harry Plunkett Greene. MacMillan, London, 1912, reprinted 1948.

For insights into musical styles and interpretation, read the song analyses in:
The Art of Accompanying by Robert Spillman. Schirmer Books, New York, NY, 1985.

More important than any reading: your own attendance at events when others perform. Observe thoughtfully and learn.

10 Extending Your Voice

Guiding questions: *What kinds of exercises will build my voice and make it stronger? How can I develop better breath control and learn to sing longer phrases? How can I learn to sing quick patterns, like scales and ornaments? How can I sing better low notes and better high notes?*

YOUR vocal work until now has formed good habits in the middle range, where most singing is done. The middle voice is an essential core that must sound and feel right before much work is done at the extremes of the range. This chapter suggests what steps to take when you are ready to move on to other challenges.

As you work to extend your abilities, use a balance of ambition and patience. Reach a little beyond what you can do now, because that is the way to grow. Keep an open attitude toward vocal change if your teacher asks you to try something new. But vocal growth cannot be forced by overworking the voice. If you ever reach the point of hoarseness or pain, stop and rest at least a few minutes and change the exercise.

Vocal strength

The voice is not a muscle that grows stronger in proportion to exercise. The voice gains strength, in terms of both loudness and stamina, by becoming more efficient, more effective in resonating the sound that comes from the vocal cords. While many voice students need muscular development to improve their posture and breathing, the muscles that actually produce the voice are strong enough for singing in almost everyone.

The vocal cords themselves probably do not change as a result of vocal study—a doctor who examines your vocal cords will not see any difference in them—but through the use of mental concepts your use of them will change. As you imagine the tone quality you want to sing, the vocal cords will adjust to produce the sound you want, as nearly as they can. With repeated practice the vocal cords become more finely tuned, producing the results you want more perfectly and more easily. Your tonal imagination also guides the muscles that determine the size and shape of the resonating spaces in your mouth and throat so that they become more efficient with practice.

Because your imagination guides the whole process of vocal growth, you must be aware and alert during practice. If you try to strengthen your voice by singing scales while you read a newspaper, you will only hurt your voice.

In chapter 4 we said, "Let your feelings be the key to vocal resonance." That is still good advice. Your will to communicate with others is the best motivation to increase your vocal resonance. Beyond that, there are other mental and physical techniques that have helped others increase their vocal strength; some of the most effective are described in the following paragraphs.

Mental focus aims to direct the voice toward a goal. When you throw a ball at a target, you think about the target and not about the way your arm moves. Just as your brain tells your arm how to throw, it will tell your vocal muscles how to make a tone reach listeners at the back of an auditorium. This is why the advice in the previous paragraph works. Of course, it is not your breath that blows the voice to the other end of the room, rather it is the sound waves, set in motion by your voice, that travel across a distance.

Mental focus works in other ways, also. Some singers improve their vocal cord function by *visualizing* the smooth, complete contact of the vocal cords as if watching them on a screen.

Mental focus is also used by many singers in the form called *voice placement*. Most good singers feel concentrated vibrations that they associate with their best tones. These sensations are results, rather than causes, of good tone; but by recalling the sensations, singers can often reproduce the good singing that went along with them.

Steady breath supply is a prerequisite for focusing the tone, and often a weak tone can be reinforced by improving the breath supply. Singing on sustained, buzzing consonants is an excellent way to assure that the breath supply is steady and energetic. Especially good are the voiced consonants [z] and [ʒ, made with the sides of the tongue touching the upper teeth so that air is directed through a narrow channel toward the front teeth.

A physical trick that often helps students increase their resonance is this: with your thumbs resting on each side of your jaw, let the tips of your longest fingers meet in front of the bridge of your nose. This forms a little "porch" in front of your face; keep your elbows down and arms relaxed so that the porch is not too wide. When you sing into the "porch," you will feel more willing to let the tone go free and more aware of any times when the tone is not free. When you take your hands away, try to achieve the same sensations of vocal freedom.

Improving breath control

Breath control always improves as vocal tone becomes more concentrated. Good tone is efficient, that is, maximum resonance is produced with a minimum amount of air. Because this is so, many good teachers, after the first few lessons, say little or nothing about breathing, feeling that good breath support will occur automatically when tonal concepts are correct.

If your breathing does not respond automatically to the demands you make, there are various technical ways to work. Begin with awareness of what your upper body is doing; let a friend examine the action of your ribs and abdomen and report the results.

- Do your lower ribs expand, including the lower back?
- Do the abdominal muscles relax outward to let breath flow in?
- Do the lower ribs remain expanded when you begin to sing?
- Do you support the singing tone with energized abdominal muscles?

These questions merely review the lessons learned in chapter 3.

Centuries ago, singers discovered a test for efficient tone production: Hold a lighted candle a few inches in front of your open mouth while you sing a vowel. If the candle flickers, too much air is escaping. Try it. When you can vocalize without making the candle flame waver, you will understand that good singing takes much less air than one would think.

"Drink the tone in" is an example of a mental concept that singers use to economize their breath. "Smell a rose" also serves that purpose. Even though air is leaving the body, the thought of air coming into the body slows the rate of movement.

Air movement is slower when the diaphragm exerts a downward pull against the inward pull of the abdominals, slowing down their motion. One way to sense this is to sing while lying on your back on the floor. Use an inch-thick paperback book to pillow your head, and sing as normally as possible. You will be more aware of the inward movement of the abdominals, helped by gravity when you are lying down, and more aware of diaphragmatic energy that keeps the abdomen from collapsing.

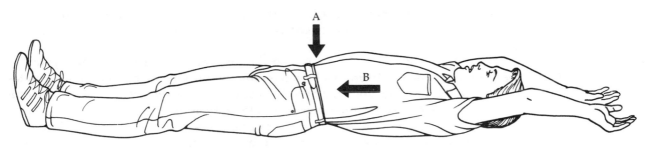

If you sing lying down, gravity (A) draws your abdomen toward the floor. Your diaphragm resists the fall of the abdominal organs (in the same direction as arrow B) in order to make room for breath.

Another trick singers use is to wear an elastic belt that pulls in the abdomen. Instead of pulling the abdomen in more quickly, the belt energizes the muscles to resist collapse. Sporting-good stores sell an elastic "tummy trimmer" to be worn while exercising. It is about seven inches wide and is fastened with Velcro so that it fits anyone.

Flexibility

Many styles of music require flexibility, the ability to sing notes rapidly. This ability does not belong just to opera singers; folk and gospel singers also use quick flourishes of notes that one must practice to acquire. In some musical styles a singer sings only the written notes, but other styles allow freedom to improvise and add ornaments at will.

Figure 10.1

Certain standardized "ornaments" have been compared to the compulsory figures practiced by ice skaters. The most basic ornament is alternation between a melody note and the note above it, called the "upper neighbor." Figure 10.1 shows an example of an upper neighbor (UN) and some common variations based on it.

Learning to sing rapidly has this in common with gaining vocal strength: The main ingredient is your musical imagination. If you can form a quick ornament clearly in your mind, your brain will tell your voice how to sing it.

Range

I have never yet met a student who had a small vocal range, but many who thought they did. The reason why students limit themselves to a small range is that they feel unsure of new sensations and unfamiliar tones. They need confidence and guidance to learn to accept their full vocal range.

Your voice almost certainly has a range of two octaves or more (unless there is a problem that deserves medical treatment, such as nodules). Your full range probably extends to three octaves, if you include the lightest high tones, falsetto in men and "whistle tones" in women (which seem useless for singing but play an important role in extending your range), and the lowest tones (even the soft breathy ones below the normal chest tones).

How much of your range can you use for singing songs? The answer depends on:

- the amount of freedom your vocal mechanism has when it adjusts to register changes;
- the musical styles you prefer to sing and whether they use a wide range; and
- your personal willingness to accept the sounds that are natural to various registers of your voice.

Low notes

If you speak at a pitch that is near the low end of your vocal range, your low notes probably already feel stronger and more comfortable than higher notes. If this is the case, you may find that vocal study changes your lower voice only a little, while your upper voice develops a great deal.

To reach the maximum power of your low notes, you may need no more than a few reminders to focus and use your tonal energy. (Even a natural bass may feel shy about using the strong low notes that are his special gift.) Often, however, young women hesitate to use chest tones, feeling that they are rough or ugly or unmusical.

One way to discover how much energy the chest voice needs is to speak the words of a song vigorously and then to concentrate on the same physical sensations while singing the same words.

Another way to learn about the chest voice is to use a deliberately ugly, "brassy" sound in the syllable "quack."

Exercises

10.1 *Quack-quack.* Use lots of energy. There is no way to make this sound beautiful, so have fun with it. Move your jaw, lips, and tongue freely, without tension. Transpose the pattern to several different keys in the lower part of your range. Practice this for only a few minutes at a time.

[kwæ kwæ kwæ kwæ kwæ kwæ kwæ kwæ   kwæ   k]

When either women or men vocalize to strengthen the resonance of low notes, it is important to use a bright tone quality and to maintain posture. Lowering your head does not help, it merely restricts the freedom of the throat.

10.2 *Low Scale and Turn.* Look straight ahead and keep your posture. Sing very legato and drop the jaw well. After the 4-note scale, observe the rest, but do not take breath; sing the *turn* on the same breath. Purpose: to focus resonance for the lowest tones.

[i   a   i   a   a _____   i   a   i   a   a _____]

High notes

High notes develop more noticeably than low notes for many students simply because the high voice has not been used much and it responds quickly to encouragement. It may even feel as if the low notes become weaker as you develop the highs, but this is an illusion. The low voice simply has less growing to do.

If high tones come easily to you, accept the gift with thanks and use it with pleasure. They require more time and practice for some people because of the fine adjustment needed between breath energy and precise function of the vocal cords.

One of the biological functions of the vocal cords is to close tightly whenever we do something that puts the breath under pressure, as in lifting a heavy weight. When the vocal cords sense a rush of air under pressure, a reflex closes them tightly to hold back the air. A singer has to overcome this natural reflex so that the vocal cords gently close the right amount for singing; they must not clutch and stop the airflow entirely.

Upper tones can be found gently with exercises 1.7 through 1.9 from chapter 1. Try singing them without taking a pitch from the piano; sing a high pitch first, then find out what it was. This tells you what the voice can sing spontaneously, instead of trying to force the voice to sing tones that it may not be ready for. When you have sung a comfortable high note, whatever it is, vocalize downward a few times. When you repeat this process, you may find that the voice has warmed up and is ready for a somewhat higher note. You can also do this with any of the hum-consonants or with the "Bubble" used in exercise 2.6.

Many singers start an exercise in a low key and move it up a half step at a time. If you do this, go only as high as you can sing with a feeling of freedom and ease in your throat. Your enthusiasm may lead you to try notes for which the throat has to tighten, and this simply leads to problems later. If this happens, rest for at least a few seconds and then start over with a different exercise.

Consider this quotation from a voice teacher of long experience, Oren Brown: "Take only what the voice gives you." And here is another that he has said often: "Think the tone and let it happen."

A successful way to discover and practice high notes is the "Open-mouth Hum," discovered and described by another prominent voice teacher, the late Dr. Berton Coffin. It resembles an [m]-hum, but without the disadvantage of having the mouth closed. After you learn it in the next exercise, you can use it to practice any other exercise or song, especially with high notes.

Exercises

10.3 *Open-mouth Hum.* Sing [hʌ], but cover your mouth completely either with the palm of your hand or with the back of your hand. No air should escape from your mouth; the air and the tone pass through your nose as in an [m]-hum. Repeat the phrase with your mouth open. Purpose: to discover a light, free approach to higher notes.

(Open-mouth hum)   [hʌ]

Singing "behind the hand" can be used to practice any vowel and any musical phrase. It has helped many women to discover "whistle" or "flageolet" tones on "High C" and above. These tones are very small at first, but some whistle voices develop to usable strength.

10.4 *Two-octave Scale.* Sing very softly on [i] or any vowel that is easy for you. If the voice breaks or skips notes at the register changes, start over more softly. Find at least one key in which you can do this scale with a free throat. Purpose: to learn to pass through register changes smoothly and easily.

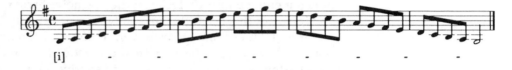

[i]   -   -   -   -   -   -   -

10.5 *Three Scales—3 + 5 + 9.* Sing the three scales separately at first. Later, combine them into one long phrase. Practice at various volume levels, not always loud or always soft. Purpose: to exercise the voice quickly and lightly through a wider range, while building flexibility.

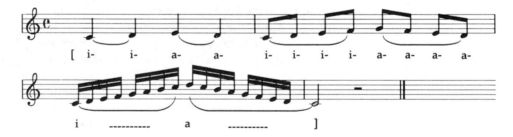

[i-   i-   a-   a-   i-   i-   i-   i-   a-   a-   a-   a-

i ---------- a ----------]

10.6 *Legato Chords.* Sing very smoothly. Feel a special continuity between the contrasting vowels [i] and [ɔ] Close [ɔ] to [o] on notes where that seems easier for you. Purpose: to exercise higher tones on dark vowels.

ɑ   ɛ   i   ɔ   u   u   ɔ   i   ɛ   ɑ

Additional reading *For proof that there are many paths to success, read the intriguing and often contradictory beliefs of opera stars in: Great Singers on Great Singing by Jerome Hines. Doubleday, Garden City, NY, 1982.*

Dozens of exercises for range extension are given in:
    Coffin's Overtones of Bel Canto by Berton Coffin. Scarecrow Press, Metuchen, NJ, 1980.

11 Understanding Your Vocal Instrument

Guiding questions: *Physically, how does the voice work? How can I keep it healthy?*

The voice as a musical instrument

All musical instruments have three common elements:

- a *motor*, which provides and transmits energy;
- a *vibrator*, which converts the energy into audible vibrations (musical pitches); and
- a *resonator*, which strengthens the tones and modifies them by selectively strengthening certain overtones.

In many cases part of the musician's body provides one of the three basic elements. In the case of a trumpet, for instance, the player's breath is the motor and the player's lips are the vibrator, while the brass tubing forms the resonator. What are the three basic elements in a violin? a guitar? a clarinet? a bass drum? a piano?

The human voice has a fourth element, an articulator, which forms consonant sounds. No other instrument can produce words. Even without the power of articulation, the vocal instrument is still the most expressive instrument for transmitting mood or emotion because of its wide variety of tone colors. Because articulation adds the advantage of exact meaning and poetic appeal, the voice has great potential to communicate emotions.

All four elements of the voice must coordinate perfectly to produce the freest, most expressive tone. They are:

1. *Motor*, or actuator: breath pressure, coming from the lungs.
2. *Vibrators*: vocal bands or cords, located in the larynx. They are set in motion by breath pressure, reacting to it in various ways owing to the action of muscles in and around the larynx.
3. *Resonators*: the entire passageway from the vocal cords up to the lips and nose. The largest flexible, therefore alterable, resonators are the pharynx and mouth. Inflexible resonators include the nasal passages and sinuses. Acoustical science has not yet answered all of our questions about resonance, including the roles played, if any, by the sinuses in the head and by the air passages below the vocal cords.
4. *Articulators*: the flexible tongue and lips acting against the inflexible teeth and hard palate, subject also to the angle of the jaw.

Chapter 2 dealt with the motor, and chapter 7 dealt with the articulators. This chapter deals with the vibrator and the resonators.

What's behind your Adam's apple?

When all goes well, we sing without knowing or thinking anything about our throats. However, the time may come when we are sick or we feel other vocal problems, and then it is wise to know the most important parts of the vocal instrument and how they work. You can easily learn about them with the help of Figure 11.1, referenced by numbers all through the following explanations.

Air from the lungs rises through the right and left bronchial tubes, which join to form the *windpipe* (trachea, #1). These air passages are stiffened by rings of cartilage that hold them open all the time. Just above your breastbone you can probably feel the bumpy surface of your windpipe. The top *ring cartilage* (cricoid cartilage, #2) is larger than the rest, and forms the base of the voice box (*larynx*, #3).

Practice saying the word "larynx" (rhymes with "fair inks") and its plural, "larynges." Most men's and some women's larynges project enough to form an "Adam's apple," which can be seen and felt. Some women have smaller larynges that are difficult to feel because they are scarcely larger than the rest of the wind-pipe.

The part of the larynx that can be felt under the skin is the *shield cartilage* (thyroid, #4), named both for its shape, as seen from the front, and its vital function of protecting the top of the air passage from collapse. Without it, we could be strangled by a tight collar or any other pressure at the front of the neck. The shield cartilage has two sides that meet in front, forming the firm tip of the Adam's apple.

Figure 11.1

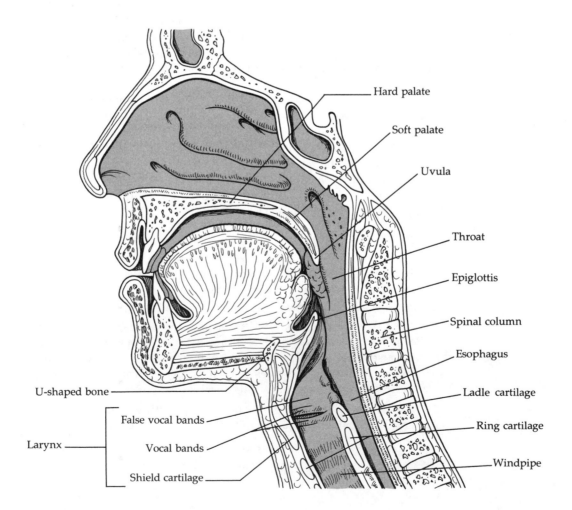

- Hard palate
- Soft palate
- Uvula
- Throat
- Epiglottis
- Spinal column
- Esophagus
- Ladle cartilage
- Ring cartilage
- Windpipe
- U-shaped bone
- False vocal bands
- Vocal bands
- Larynx
- Shield cartilage

The forward ends of the vocal bands are attached to the inside surface of the shield cartilage. They stretch over the top of the open windpipe, and at the rear end they are attached to two smaller cartilages, the right and left *ladle cartilages* (arytenoids, located at #5 but hidden in the tissue). The ladles slide along the upper surface of the ring cartilage. Thanks to a complex system of muscles, the ladles are able to move together and apart and can tip either forward and back or to the side, always moving counter to each other. Together they determine whether the rear ends of the vocal bands are close or far apart. The vocal bands are always close to each other at the front ends, but the arytenoids pull them apart at the rear when we breathe in and bring them together again when we speak or sing.

The ring, the shield, and the two ladles form the stiff framework of the larynx. Being cartilages, they are flexible in children, harden as we mature, and eventually turn to bone. This is one of several reasons why voice quality changes with age. The inner surfaces of the larynx are covered with *mucus membrane*. When it is irritated by infection, you have "laryngitis" and you may lose your voice.

What really interests us are the *vocal bands* (#6). The mass of the vocal bands consists of the thyro-arytenoid muscles (named for the cartilages where their ends are attached). Their edges, where the finest adjustments for singing take place, are formed of a white membrane that also covers their undersurfaces. More about them later.

Just above the vocal bands are two similar bands, called the *false vocal bands* (#7). It is not clear whether they play a role in voice production, but the space between the true and the false cords may be a significant resonator.

Directly behind the larynx is the top of the *food pipe* (esophagus, #8), which is closed flat against the *spinal column* (#9) except when something passes through it, going to the stomach.

On the way to the esophagus, food and drink have to cross over the larynx without falling in. Therefore, the top of the larynx is guarded by a leaf-shaped cartilage, the *epiglottis* (#10). Attached to the upper front edge of the shield cartilage, the epiglottis stands nearly upright most of the time, then falls down and back when we swallow, completely covering the larynx.

The *U-shaped bone* (hyoid, #11) is located above the larynx at the base of the tongue; you may be able to feel the ends of it on either side of your neck just below the jaw. It forms part of the framework from which the larynx is suspended. You can sense this flexible suspension system if you use the backs of your fingers on either side of your larnyx and push it a little bit from side to side.

The open space that forms our main resonator for singing is the *throat* (pharynx, #12). When you yawn in front of the mirror, you can see the back wall of the oral pharynx, so-called because it is closely connected to your mouth. If your pharynx is irritated by infection, you have pharyngitis, which is often painful but does not always involve losing your voice. The open space extends upward to form the naso-pharynx, which is closely connected to the nasal passages.

When you are looking in the mirror to find your pharynx, you can't help noticing your *uvula* (Latin for "little grape," #13), which hangs down from the *soft palate* (#14). You will notice that the soft palate can move up and down quite far. It may hang down so far that your uvula is hidden behind your tongue and you cannot see into the pharynx at all, or it can rise up to expose quite a bit of the pharynx.

As you see, the soft palate can change the size and shape of the pharynx considerably. Also, by rising and lowering, it determines how much breath goes out through your nose and how much through your mouth. If your soft palate is too low, too much of your breath moves through the nose, and your tone sounds nasal. If your soft palate is too high, it can seal off the nasal passage so that you cannot say [m] or [n], and you sound like a person stopped-up with a cold. Some people habitually sing with the soft palate too high, resulting in a dull, indistinct sound. Most voice teachers recommend keeping the palate high but not closing off the nasal passages.

In front of the soft palate is the bony *hard palate* (#15). By running your tongue back along the roof of your mouth you can feel where the hard palate ends.

Over the palate is the space called the nasal passages. The left and right passages are separated by a bony partition (septum). The sides of the nasal passages are lined with irregular projections that serve, like the surface of a radiator, to warm the air as it goes by.

Other parts of the vocal mechanism—the tongue, lips, jaw, and teeth—are all familiar and visible.

Vocal health

As a basis for understanding vocal health, let's focus more closely on the vocal bands themselves. Figure 11.2 shows how they look in the dental mirror that a laryngologist uses to look down your throat. The vocal bands are seen while closing to make a sound, but not yet fully closed.

Figure 11.2

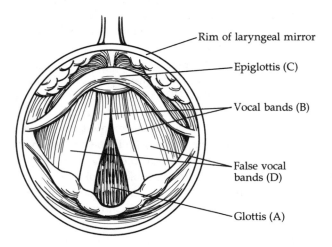

- Rim of laryngeal mirror
- Epiglottis (C)
- Vocal bands (B)
- False vocal bands (D)
- Glottis (A)

At the center of the picture is a shaded space, the glottis (A), looking down into the windpipe. On either side of the glottis are the vocal bands (B). Because this is a mirror image, the point where the vocal bands meet at the front of the larynx is toward the top of the picture but out of sight, hidden underneath the erect epiglottis (C). The rear end of the vocal bands is toward the bottom of the picture, also out of sight. The vocal bands are white and smooth when they are rested and healthy, pinkish after vigorous use. They turn red and swollen when you have laryngitis. To either side of the white vocal bands, we see the pink upper surface of the false vocal cords (D), which conceal most of the body of the vocal cords.

Here are some essential facts about the vocal cords:

1. The vocal cords are tiny muscles. To visualize them, think of a soprano's vocal cords stretched over a round opening with about the same diameter as a dime. A bass's vocal cords are stretched over an opening the size of a nickel. We ask these small muscles to do remarkable feats for us.

2. On most tones in your range, your vocal cords touch each other and separate again, once for each vibration. For instance, if you sing middle C, a pitch that is in everyone's range, your vocal cords touch each other 262 times per second. They also part 262 times per second and let 262 puffs of air escape, initiating a wave movement in the air. A listener hears this wave as a tone with the pitch we call middle C and a frequency of 262 Hz.

If a man sings the C below middle C, the cords touch each other only 131 times per second, but if a woman sings the C above middle C, there are 524 such events. A soprano's high C has 1048 vibrations, but at that speed the cords probably do not really touch each other. Can you imagine how many thousands of times the cords contact each other in a musical phrase or in a whole song? Clearly, if there is anything rough, inefficient, or unnecessarily forceful about the singing tone, the contact edges of the vocal cords will be subjected to considerable friction, even chafing.

3. Like the diaphragm, the vocal cords have no proprioceptive nerves, no way to tell us when they are in trouble. Nature wants to assure that the vocal cords do the best work they can, never shying away from pain. Any throat pain that we experience comes from overworked muscles or infected tissues around the cords but not from the cords themselves.

4. When our vocal cords are abused or infected, the body seeks to heal them by sending extra liquids to the scene: extra mucus to cover their surfaces and extra blood to heal any internal damage done. Increased blood supply turns the vocal cords pink or red, and they get larger.

5. When the cords swell slightly, the first sign of trouble may be hoarseness, meaning that the edges of the cords are not closing perfectly and air is escaping between them. They may be unable to form the thin edges needed for high tones. If we persist in trying to talk and sing, we develop pain, as nearby muscles strain to take over the work of the vocal cords. If the vocal cords swell too much, their edges become bumpy, perhaps unable to meet and form tones at all. Then we lose our voices and have to rest them until the swelling goes down.

Vocal overuse

The facts you have learned about the vocal cords explain why *overuse causes more voice problems than any other factor.* Enthusiastic, energetic singers love to socialize and enjoy expressing their emotions. It's not surprising that many of us overuse our voices.

What does "overuse" mean? The medical term is "hyperfunction," and it includes:

- shouting, for instance, cheering at a sports event;
- loud talking and laughing, for instance, at a noisy party;
- insistent talking, as when we try to dominate others;
- talking or singing over the noise of a moving car or other machinery;
- coughing and throat clearing, which violently rub the bands against each other;
- singing at an inappropriate pitch level, as when one is placed in the wrong section of a choir;
- singing longer and louder than we can do with comfort, whether that means singing with a rock band or getting carried away at an exciting choral rehearsal.

The limits of safe vocal use differ a great deal from one individual to another. Most of us learn our limits by the unhappy experience of hoarseness or temporary voice loss. Fortunately, our vocal cords are resilient; with enough rest, they usually repair themselves. We only need to be aware of trouble signs and stop doing whatever is causing the abuse.

I love to cheer at a football game, but if I can't sing for three or four days afterward, was the fun worth it?

A damaged voice

You have learned how and why the vocal cords swell up to protect and heal themselves in cases of overuse. If overuse continues and the cords do not get enough rest to repair themselves, a persistent bump called a vocal nodule or vocal node may develop on the edge of one or both cords. Nodes prevent the cords from closing correctly and cause reduction of range and volume. *Only a physician can correctly diagnose vocal nodes.*

If you experience persistent hoarseness, consult a physician to find out whether you have nodes and what treatment you need. In the early stages nodes are soft; they often heal with a few weeks of rest and reduced voice use. In later stages they grow progressively harder and require more rest to heal. Very seldom will a physician recommend surgical removal. (Never undertake surgery without a second or third medical opinion.)

If your cords develop nodes, don't necessarily blame your voice teacher, who sees you only a short time each week and cannot possibly monitor all your activities. Your physician can recommend a speech therapist who will help you to identify vocally abusive habits in your daily life and replace them with healthful ones.

Avoiding more colds

Colds and influenzas are caused by a variety of viruses; we can be immunized against some of them, but not all. Viruses are transmitted through the air when people cough and sneeze, but often they are introduced into our respiratory system by our own hands. When you shake hands with someone or hold the handle on the seat of a bus, you have no idea what viruses may be present. Wash your hands regularly and keep them away from your eyes, nose, lips, and mouth.

When you have been exposed to a virus, keep your first line of respiratory defense strong: *Keep your vocal tract moist.*

Your entire vocal tract is lined with mucous membrane, which produces moisture. We tend to notice mucus only when sickness has made it thick and annoying, but the constant, unnoticed production of mucus is essential to our health and comfort. Particles of foreign matter and microorganisms that land on mucous membrane stick to the wet surface and are carried away on the cleansing stream of moisture. If the membrane is dry, foreign particles are in irritating contact with body tissue and microorganisms have an opportunity to attack.

Heated and air-conditioned buildings, as well as automobiles and airplanes, usually have air that is unnaturally dry. Regular use of an ultrasonic vaporizer, especially in the room where you sleep, may save you from many respiratory infections. It also helps to drink lots of liquids, especially water of a medium temperature. Avoid diuretics, like coffee, which drain moisture from our tissues.

While keeping your humidity high, you can also keep your immunity as high as possible with reasonable rest, avoidance of stress, good nourishment that includes vitamin C, and, yes, a good mental attitude. Avoid letting your body become chilled because viruses thrive at a temperature somewhat lower than our normal body temperature. After long exposure to cold, a warm bath or shower may help raise your resistance.

Tobacco smoke obviously dries out our throat tissues. Marijuana smoke is even hotter because it is unfiltered. Don't smoke. Problems with cocaine and crack have been described by Dr. Van Lawrence in *The NATS Journal*.

If, in spite of all your care, you still catch a cold, drink liquids, rest, and reduce the amount you use your voice. Use caution with respect to medication. If you lose your voice, no magic potion will restore it. Remember that antihistamines, which stop your nose from running, also dry your throat.

Be aware that aspirin and products that contain aspirin dilate the capillaries that supply blood to the throat tissues, introducing the possibility that the thin walls of the dilated capillaries can rupture and hemorrhage. Throat specialists recommend non-aspirin products for pain relief for singers.

As for singing and voice lessons while you have a cold, follow your teacher's advice. If vocal rest is in order, that means:

- talking quietly and less than usual;
- no singing, shouting, or laughing;
- no whistling or loud whispering, both of which use the vocal cords.

For any vocal disorder that lasts more than three or four days, see a physician who will examine your vocal cords. Before your office visit, restudy the vocal anatomy described earlier in this chapter. By being an informed patient you can ask better questions and help the doctor to help you.

Additional reading.   *The grandfather of voice books, now revised and in its second quarter century:*
Keep Your Voice Healthy by Friedrich Brodnitz, M.D. College-Hill Press, 2nd ed., 1987.

Van L. Lawrence, M.D., and Robert T. Sataloff, M.D., contribute an invaluable column on vocal health to The NATS Journal, published by the National Association of Teachers of Singing. Over a period of years these articles have provided current information on a wide variety of vocal and medical questions. These journals can be found in your local public or college library.

[handwritten notes:]

① HIGH MOISTURE

Prevention: water

    not milk or Dairy
    not alcohol (takes away moisture)
     or Caffeine

② HIGH IMMUNITY — flu shots
     wash hands
     minimise stress
     rest
     balanced diet
     physically fit
     good mental attitude

③ USING THE VOICE WISELY

12 Notes for Nonmusicians

Guiding questions: *Do I have a "musical ear"? What vocabulary is necessary to communicate with other musicians? What does "in a key" mean? What is a scale? How do musicians think about rhythm? What is a measure? What is syncopation? What can I learn from looking at a piece of printed music?*

THIS chapter comes last in the book because you do not need it if you already know the vocabulary of music. If you do need this chapter, read it on your own outside of class or whenever your teacher assigns it.

When I meet a new acquaintance and mention that I teach singing, that person often responds by saying something about a lack of musical background. Here are some things people say and some answers I like to give if the other person seems willing to listen:

"Oh, I don't know a thing about music!" *Yes, you do. You are familiar with a tremendous amount of music. You just need a vocabulary to talk about it.*

"I hated piano lessons when I was a kid, but now I wish I'd kept on with them." *Don't feel guilty about your childhood music lessons. If music has a high enough priority for you, you can still learn.*

"I'd love to sing, but my family all say I have a tin ear." *Sing anyway, and enjoy it. When you find the right group of people to sing with, you will fit right in.*

You do not need to apologize because other people had music lessons or home experiences that you did not have. Whatever you learn, starting now, will enrich your life through increased awareness of the music all around you.

What is a musical ear?

The person who worries about having a "tin ear" might like to know that musicians do not all have a mysterious faculty that others lack. Everyone has a "musical ear" to some degree. Like other mental skills, the ability to remember and reproduce musical pitches is highly individual; it varies a great deal from person to person, and it improves with training.

A very few persons have so-called "perfect pitch," which means the ability to hear any pitch and call it by the correct name or to sing any note at will. Most professional musicians have some degree of "relative pitch," which means an ability to recognize or to sing particular notes with some reliability. Neither perfect nor relative pitch is essential for you to learn to sing melodies easily and correctly. All you need is an ability to hear several tones in a row and sing them back accurately.

Are you "tone-deaf"? No; probably no physically normal person is tone-deaf. It is contradictory that people call themselves tone-deaf when they are perfectly able to hear the difference between two melodies and even to hear wrong notes or out of tune notes. People who believe that they are tone-deaf simply have not developed the ear-to-brain-to-throat coordination that singing requires. Occasionally, a "pitch problem" disappears as soon as the student realizes what vocal register to use; other cases require more time and experience in a supportive group-singing environment.

Pitch

When Maria in *The Sound of Music* started to teach music to the von Trapp children, she made up a song, "Do-Re-Mi," page 97. The seven syllables *Do, Re, Mi, Fa, So, La, Ti,* are widely used names for the notes that we call C, D, E, F, G, A, B. Because we hear tones as being "higher" and "lower," it makes sense to arrange the names of the tones vertically, like this:

8	C	Do
7	B	Ti
6	A	La
5	G	So
4	F	Fa
3	E	Mi
2	D	Re
1	C	Do

Sing up a scale, starting from the lowest note and singing "One, two, three. . . ." (Whether or not you start on C is not important right now.) Sing back down the scale: "Eight, seven, six. . . ." (It sounds like the Christmas song "Joy to the World.") Sing up and down the scale again, singing letter names: "C, D, E. . . ." Sing up and down a third time, singing the names of the syllables: "Do, Re, Mi. . . ." Now you will see the connections between Maria's song and the notes that we call a *C major scale.*

The C major scale is written like this, using alternate lines and spaces of a musical staff.

C   D   E   F   G   A   B   C   B   A   G   F   E   D   C

If you have a keyboard, you can easily play this scale. The black keys are in groups of two and three; any white key that is immediately to the left of a group of two black keys is a C. Start there and play the white keys in order from left to right until you reach the next C; you will hear an ascending scale. Play them again from right to left; you will hear a descending scale. The distance

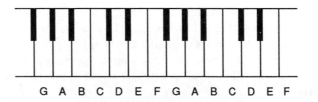

G A B C D E F G A B C D E F

between two neighboring notes is called a scale step, but not all scale steps are equal. You can see that between some pairs of white keys there is a black key, but there is none between others because they already sound as close to each other as notes can sound in our musical system. The smallest distance between notes is called a half-step; it is the distance between adjacent keys, whether white or black. Most scale steps are a whole-step apart, which is the distance between two keys that have another one, white or black, between them.

Do is at both the bottom and the top of our scale because the series repeats itself both upward and downward, as high and as low as your ear can hear. Below *Do* there is always another *Ti;* above *Do* there is always another *Re.*

What is the relationship between the lower *Do* and the higher one? They are different notes, but they sound so much alike that they have the same name. Why? The vibrations of the upper *Do* are exactly twice as fast as those of the lower one. If you play them together, every second vibration of the upper *Do* will coincide with a vibration of the lower *Do.* (You don't hear separate vibrations because they are much too fast. See the frequencies of various C's on page 83.)

The distance between the two *Do's* is an *octave* (from Latin *octo,* eight). In a voice class it is important to realize that women and men usually sing an octave apart. If women sing *in unison,* they all sing the same notes at the same time. If we say that a mixed group of people sing in unison, we are overlooking the fact that women and men are actually singing an octave apart. When men sing the songs in this book, they sound an octave lower than the notes are written. (Tenors in choir also sing an octave lower than their music is written.) If your teacher is of the opposite sex from you, you may need some practice before you can recognize and sing back the pitches that she or he sings for you.

Sometimes singers avoid the extremes of their range by changing a song, singing a few notes or a phrase an octave higher or an octave lower than written. At other times singers change notes just to use the extremes of their range, especially to make the ending of a song more exciting by singing it high.

Whole-steps and half-steps are also known as seconds, and the other *intervals* (distances between notes) have simple numerical names: a third, a fourth, etc. Each interval has its distinctive sound and with practice you can learn to recognize them, but it is not necessary right now. For the present, you may learn your songs "by rote," that is, by hearing them repeatedly.

Keys

Sometimes a student asks, "What key is good for my voice?" First, we have to talk about what "in a key" means, and why the question has to be answered for each separate song.

Most pieces of music reach a point of finality at the end. If the piece were interrupted, you would be dissatisfied. Test this by asking someone to play "Auld Lang Syne" on the piano (the first 8m are enough) and stop without playing the last note. There is a sense of incompleteness, even frustration.

Even if you were hearing the song for the first time, you would know intuitively what note to expect at the end. You know this because you have heard thousands of pieces of music written in what is called the *tonal system.* The final note and the chord that is based on that note are both called *tonic,* and you can think of this word as meaning "home base." Test this concept again by having "Auld Lang Syne" played with a "wrong" chord at the end! In fact, soon after the piece begins, you already have a sense of what the correct final chord should be.

If we say that a song is "in the key of F," that is a way of saying that we expect the final note and final chord to be F. There's an easy way to experience differences in keys: Sing through "Auld Lang Syne," remember the final note, and start on that note to sing the song again. If you succeed, you will find yourself singing in a new key, a fourth higher than the first one. Is the new key comfortable? If it is too high, then you have quickly learned how important it is to have a song in a comfortable key.

Most people are comfortable singing "Do-Re-Mi" in the key of C (some need it a little higher or lower). The range is from C to C. Notice that if you start singing "Auld Lang Syne" on C, the range is the same except for one extra note,

D. Is the final note C? No; it is F. This shows that songs that are in your comfortable range are not necessarily all in the same key.

This is why the student's question mentioned earlier could not be answered easily: songs may have the same high notes and low notes and yet have different tonics.

The notes of the C major scale are not the only notes in our musical system. Other notes were discovered because of our need to sing in other keys, a rather complicated concept that took centuries of musical history to develop.

Here is a simple example: when we begin a scale on F, we want the third and fourth notes to be a half-step apart, so that the scale will sound similar to the C major scale. Since the third note is A, the fourth note must be B-flat, the note that is a half-step higher than A. Musical notation shows this by placing a symbol called a flat at the beginning of the piece; the flat changes every written B in the piece to a B-flat. An F scale looks like this:

All major scales are built on the same principle, having half-steps between notes 3 and 4 and notes 7 and 8 and whole steps between the others. It is by hearing this pattern, even if you are unaware of it, that you recognize the tonic of a major key.

Just as a flat sign lowers a note by a half-step, a sharp sign raises a note by a half-step. A-sharp (a half-step higher than A) looks different from B-flat (a half-step lower than B), but sounds exactly the same. Each of the black keys on a keyboard has two names, a sharp name and a flat name.

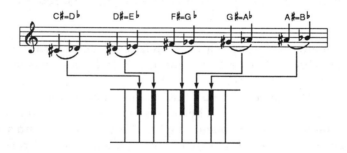

Since A-sharp (A♯) and B-flat (B♭) sound exactly the same when played on the piano, why do they have different names? Because they are used in the context of different scales, which will be very confusing to read if they are not written systematically.

The seven tones of C major plus the five tones that are played by black keys make a total of twelve tones in every octave. Played in order, the twelve tones form the *chromatic scale*. Any of the twelve can serve as the tonic of a key. This *tonal system* is typical of *Western music,* defined as the dominant artistic music of Western Europe and the Western Hemisphere. Other cultures—for instance, Chinese and Hindu—have evolved other musical systems of music with their own special features.

The great strength of Western music is the flexibility of tonal music. We can even change key ("modulate") in the middle of a song, meaning that the ear can be fooled into accepting a new note as a temporary tonic. This is achieved by the use of temporary alterations of the scale, called "chromatics." When you see flats or sharps in a piece of music, something like this may be going on. If you take a course in harmony, you will learn more about this.

So far we have not mentioned *minor keys*, but they have great charm and are not always sad, as people often think. To hear a minor scale, go back to the keyboard and play a scale on white keys from A to A. This is called the natural minor scale of A minor, and its most important feature is the half-step between notes 2 and 3 (rather than 3 and 4 as in a major scale). Notes 6 and 7 are flexible in minor scales, often being raised a half-step at the composer's wish.

Rhythm

Musical rhythm is also a flexible system, primarily concerned with patterns of accents rather than with real time.

Babies notice repeated movements and sounds and respond to them with pleasure. The most primitive rhythm is simple repetition of a steady beat:

/ /

A baby notices such regularity and enjoys it, but does not respond the same way if strong beats are put in randomly, like this:

| / / | | | / / / | / | / / | / / / | / / | /

Pleasurable musical rhythm begins when the stronger beats occur in a pattern, like this four-beat pattern:

| / / / | / / / | / / / | / / / | / / / |

or this three-beat pattern:

| / / | / / | / / | / / | / / | / / |

Most of the music we hear every day is organized in patterns of two, three, or four beats. In written music, the beginning of a beat pattern is shown by a vertical line called a *measure bar* or *bar line*. The music between two bar lines is one *measure* or one *bar* of music.

The note just to the right of the bar line is always a strong beat. It is called a *downbeat*, because of the downward movement of a conductor's arm to start a measure. Often a phrase of music begins with an *upbeat*, which consists of one or two or more notes that prepare for the downbeat. Think of the melody to "He's Got the Whole World in His Hands." What word comes on the first downbeat? How many upbeat notes are there? What word comes on the second downbeat?

The diagrams of 4- and 3-beat patterns imply that downbeats are naturally louder than the beats in between, but that is not always so. When gospel singers clap, they usually clap after the downbeat, not with it. Disco music features very loud accents that are perceived as offbeat, rather than on the downbeat. Downbeats are established by means other than loudness, such as:

- patterns of notes in the accompaniment that repeat once or twice in every measure;
- chord changes on the first beat of each measure;
- word accents.

In addition to notes on the basic beats, there are notes that last more than one beat and other notes that occur faster than the basic beats. You have already noticed that notes all have oval heads. The longest note, called a whole note (normally four beats), is simply an empty oval. Adding a vertical stem makes a half-note (two beats), filling it in makes a quarter note (one beat), and each added flag cuts the length of the note in half again. Ways to produce other note lengths include: combining consecutive notes of the same pitch with a curved line called a "tie"; adding one-half to the length of a note with a dot; or bracketing three notes together with an indication that they take up the time value of two.

There can be a sense of surprise or fun when an event in the music suddenly goes against the pattern. Perhaps a strong high note comes on a beat that is normally weak and then holds over to the next strong beat. Perhaps an emphatic word occurs in a weak part of the measure; or perhaps when we expect a downbeat there is a rest instead, and the expected note comes a half-beat late. Such ways of shifting the measure accent are called *syncopation*.

Looking at music

Even if you think you "can't read music," it will be worthwhile to take a close look at the music of a song you want to learn in order to see what the printed page can tell you. As an example, let's use Schubert's "An die Musik" (To Music), on page 156.

Just below the title of the song, in German and in English, is a small musical staff that indicates pitches of the highest and lowest notes in the song. Slightly lower, on the left, are the names of the poet who wrote the words and, on the right, the composer of the music.

On the page are three *systems*, each made up of three lines of music, connected to each other by vertical lines at the left. Each line of music is written on a *staff* of five parallel lines. In each group of staves, the upper one contains the voice part with words below. The lower two staves, which are connected by all of the measure bars, are for the piano music. Most of the time the pianist's right hand plays from the upper staff and the left hand plays from the lower one, but crossovers also occur.

At the left of the upper two staves are fancy symbols called *G clefs*, meant to draw attention to the second line from the bottom; notes on this line are G's. The lowest staff has an *F clef*, formed of a curlicue and two dots, that draws attention to the fourth line; notes on this line are F's. The midpoint between the upper and lower staves is *middle C*, which is written either on a partial line below the upper staff or on a partial line above the lower staff.

Immediately after the clefs there may be flat or sharp signs called the *key signature*; these signs affect all of the notes that follow on the same line or in the same space, and they determine what key the music is in. (The key of F, illustrated above, has one flat in the signature.) The key signature is repeated on every line.

Next comes a *meter signature* or *time signature*, in this case a C with a vertical slash through it. This means that there are two beats per measure, each a half-note. A similar symbol, C without a slash, means four beats per measure, each a quarter-note. Other meter signatures consist of two numbers: The upper number tells how many beats are in a measure and the lower one tells what kind of note stands for a beat.

"An die Musik" begins with a piano *introduction*, so the voice part has rest signs in the first two measures. At the end of m2 is a double bar line with two dots to its right; later you will come back to this point and sing the music over again.

There is another rest on the downbeat of m3, meaning that you sing just afterward. You have had a chance to hear how quickly the chords move in the piano part, and you can time your notes to match them. Look at your first note, and notice that in m2 the piano played that note four times; you will have a good chance to hear it when the pianist plays the introduction.

Looking ahead at your part, you will see that there are other rests where you can take a breath, but there are not enough of them. You will need more breaths, taken at punctuation marks or wherever you can breathe without disturbing the meaning of the words. Many songs have no written rests at all; the composer assumes that you will find satisfactory places to breathe.

After the first stanza the piano plays an *interlude;* at the repeat bar (with dots to the left) the pianist goes back to m3. After the second stanza the pianist plays the interlude again, but now it is called a *postlude,* and it ends with the measure after the repeat bars.

Some folk and pop songs in this book have symbols above the vocal line to tell a pianist or guitarist what chords to play. The player decides exactly what notes to play and how to play them, and it is not considered important for the notes to be exactly the same for every performance. In classical music, chord symbols are not used because the composer has written the notes of the accompaniment with care, expecting them always to be the same.

This little introduction to musical scores may have raised more questions in your mind than it answered. At least, you have seen that the score is a kind of roadmap, a chart from which you can get useful information even if you do not play an instrument. If this chapter has awakened your curiosity, you would enjoy learning more in a course on rudiments of music or a beginning piano class.

Additional reading

For a clear, readable, thoroughly practical explanation of music symbols, based on tunes you already know:
Learn to Read Music by Howard Shanet. Simon and Schuster, 1956.

Songs

America the Beautiful

Katherine Lee Bates   Samuel A. Ward

1. O beau-ti-ful for spa-cious skies, For am-ber waves of grain, For pur-ple moun-tain
2. O beau-ti-ful for pa-triot dream That sees be-yond the years Thine al - a-bas-ter

maj - es-ties A - bove the fruit - ed plain! A - mer - i - ca! A - mer - i - ca! God
cit - ies gleam, Un - dimmed by hu - man tears!

shed His grace on thee, And crown thy good with broth-er-hood From sea to shin-ing sea!

Auld Lang Syne

Traditional   Scotland

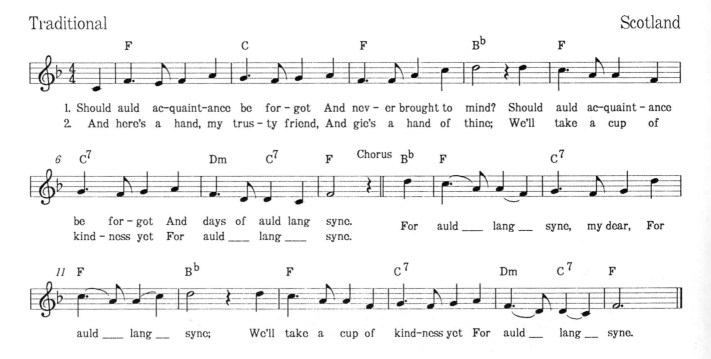

1. Should auld ac-quaint-ance be for-got And nev - er brought to mind? Should auld ac-quaint - ance
2. And here's a hand, my trus-ty friend, And gie's a hand of thine; We'll take a cup of

be for-got And days of auld lang syne. For auld ___ lang ___ syne, my dear, For
kind - ness yet For auld ___ lang ___ syne.

auld ___ lang ___ syne; We'll take a cup of kind-ness yet For auld ___ lang ___ syne.

Notes about these songs are on page 237.

Come, Follow!
(a round)

John Hilton, adapted   John Hilton, adapted

Come, fol-low, fol-low, fol-low, fol-low, fol-low, fol-low me!

Whith-er shall I fol-low, fol-low, fol-low, whith-er shall I fol-low, fol-low thee?

To the green-wood, to the green-wood, to the green-wood, green-wood tree.

Do-Re-Mi

Oscar Hammerstein II   Richard Rodgers

Doe, a deer, a fe-male deer, Ray, a drop of gol-den sun, _____

Me, a name I call my-self, Far, a long, long way to run, _____

Sew, a nee-dle pul-ling thread, _____ La, a note to fol-low sew,

Tea, a drink with jam and bread that will bring us back to do- oh-

oh- oh! do! _____ Do- re- mi- fa- so- la- ti- do! _____

Notes about these songs are on page 237.

He's Got the Whole World in His Hands

Traditional

Spiritual

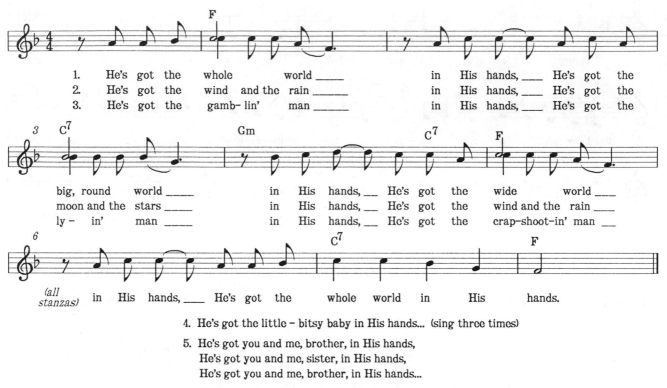

1. He's got the whole world ____ in His hands, ___ He's got the
2. He's got the wind and the rain ____ in His hands, ___ He's got the
3. He's got the gamb-lin' man ____ in His hands, ___ He's got the

big, round world ____ in His hands, __ He's got the wide world ___
moon and the stars ____ in His hands, __ He's got the wind and the rain ___
ly-in' man ____ in His hands, __ He's got the crap-shoot-in' man __

(all stanzas) in His hands, ___ He's got the whole world in His hands.

4. He's got the little - bitsy baby in His hands... (sing three times)

5. He's got you and me, brother, in His hands,
   He's got you and me, sister, in His hands,
   He's got you and me, brother, in His hands...

6. Oh, He's got everybody in His hands... (sing three times)

Hinay Ma Tov
(a round)

Psalm 133

Israel

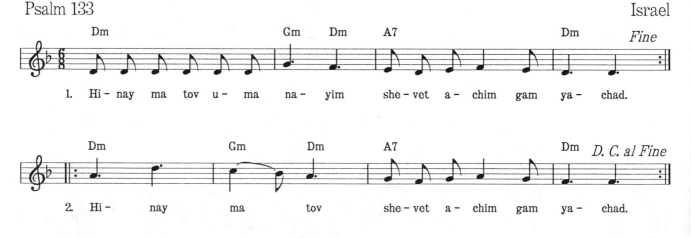

1. Hi - nay ma tov u - ma na - yim she - vet a - chim gam ya - chad.

2. Hi - nay ma tov she - vet a - chim gam ya - chad.

Literal translation: See how good and pleasant it is for brothers to dwell together!

Notes about these songs are on page 237.

Michael, Row the Boat Ashore

Traditional

Spiritual

1. Mi - chael, row the boat a - shore,
2. Sis - ter, help to trim the sails, Hal - le - lu -
3. Jor - dan's wa - ter is chil - ly and cold,

jah!
Mi - chael, row the boat a - shore, Hal - le - lu - jah!
Sis - ter, help to trim the sails, Hal - le - lu - jah!
Chills the bo - dy but not the soul,

Old Smokey

Traditional

U. S. A.

1. On top of Old Smo - key, _____ all cov - ered with
2. Now, court - in's a pleas - ure, _____ but part - in' is
3. A thief, he will rob you _____ and steal what you

snow, _____ I lost my true lov -
grief, _____ A false - heart - ed lov -
hate, _____ But a false - heart - ed lov -

er _____ by a - court - in' too slow. _____
er _____ is _ worse than a thief. _____
er _____ will _ lead you to your grave. _____

4. The grave will decay you and turn you to dust;
   Not one man in a hundred a poor girl can trust.

5. They'll hug you and kiss you and tell you more lies
   Than the cross-ties in a railroad or the stars in the skies.

Notes about these songs are on page 237.

The Star - Spangled Banner

Francis Scott Key

John Stafford Smith

Notes about this song are on page 238.

Scarborough Fair

Traditional   England

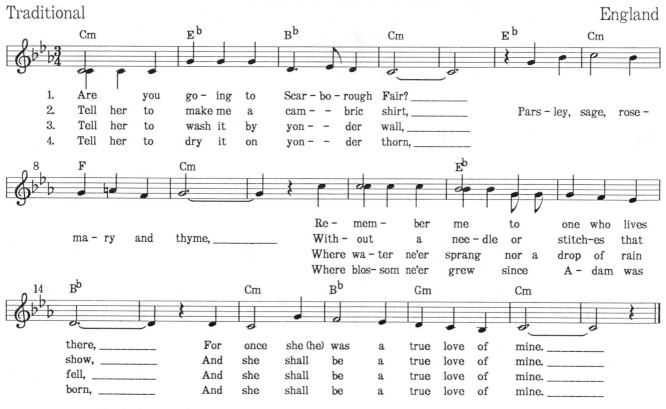

1. Are you go-ing to Scar-bo-rough Fair? _____
2. Tell her to make me a cam - - bric shirt, _____ Pars-ley, sage, rose-
3. Tell her to wash it by yon - - der wall, _____
4. Tell her to dry it on yon - - der thorn, _____

ma - ry and thyme, _____
Re - mem - ber me to one who lives
With - out a nee - dle or stitch-es that
Where wa - ter ne'er sprang nor a drop of rain
Where blos- som ne'er grew since A - dam was

there, _____ For once she (he) was a true love of mine. _____
show, _____ And she shall be a true love of mine. _____
fell, _____ And she shall be a true love of mine. _____
born, _____ And she shall be a true love of mine. _____

Text when sung by a woman:

2. Tell him to bring me an acre of land, Parsley...
   Betwixt the wild ocean and yonder sea sand, And he ...

3. Tell him to plough it with one ram's horn, Parsley...
   And sow it all over with one peppercorn, And he...

4. Tell him to reap it with a sickle of leather, Parsley ...
   And bind it together with one peacock feather, And he ....

When the Saints Go Marchin' In

Traditional   Spiritual

Oh, when the saints _____ go march-in' in, _____ Oh, when the

saints go march - in' in, _____ Oh Lord, I want to be in that

num - ber, _____ When the saints go march - in' in.

Notes about these songs are on page 238.

Aupres de ma Blonde

Traditional

Normandie, France
Arranged by John Glenn Paton

Lively

1. Au jar-din de mon pè— re Les
2. La caill', la tour-te— rel-le Et
3. Ell' chan-te pour les fil— les Qui

lau—riers sont fleu—ris; _____ Au jar-din de mon pè— re Les
la jo-li per-drix, _____ La caill', la tour-te— rel-le, Et
n'ont point de ma—ri; _____ Ell' chan-te pour les fil— les Qui

lau—riers sont fleu—ris; _____ Tous les oi-seaux du mon— de Vont
la jo-li per-drix _____ Et la blan-che co— lom-be Qui
n'ont point de ma— ri; _____ C'est pas pour moi qu'ell' chan— te, Car

Literal translation: (1) In my father's garden/ the laurels are blooming;/ birds from everywhere/ go...
(2) The quail, the turtledove,/ the pretty partridge,/ and the white dove,/ which...
(3) The dove sings for the girls/ who have no husbands,/ but it does not sing for me,/ because...

Notes about this song are on page 238.

(1) there to nest.../
(2) sings day and night.../ (Refrain) Beside my blonde wife,/ how good it is to sleep!
(3) I have a handsome one!/

Cockles and Mussels

Traditional

Ireland, ca. 1750

Arranged by V. A. C., revised by J. G. P.

Notes about this song are on page 238.

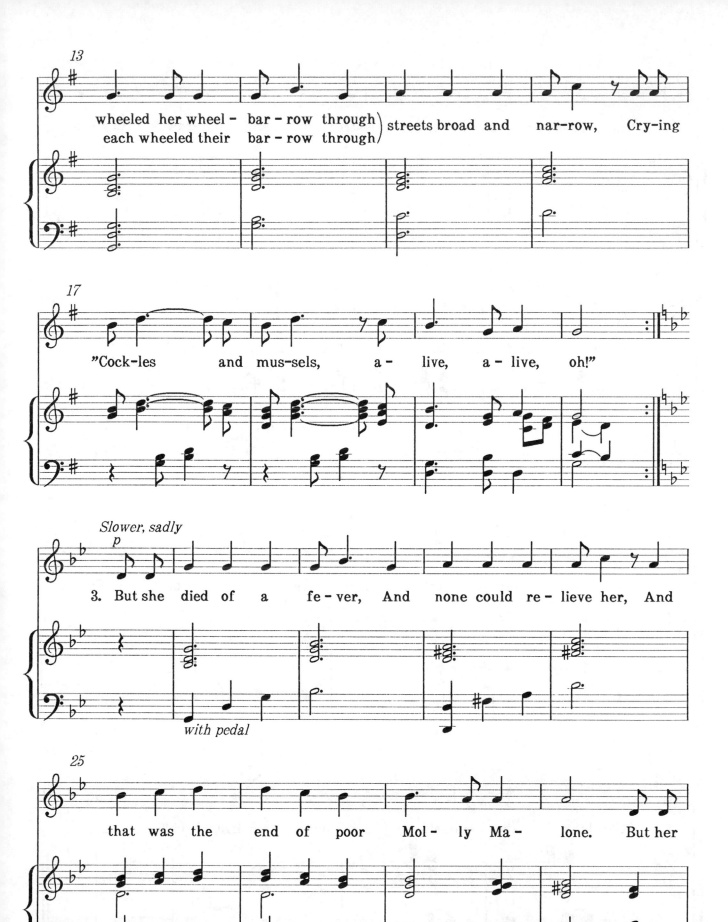

wheeled her wheel - bar - row through streets broad and nar-row, Cry-ing
each wheeled their bar - row through

"Cock-les and mus-sels, a - live, a - live, oh!"

Slower, sadly
p

3. But she died of a fe - ver, And none could re - lieve her, And

with pedal

that was the end of poor Mol - ly Ma - lone. But her

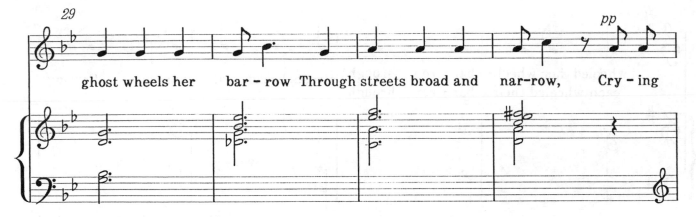

ghost wheels her bar-row Through streets broad and nar-row, Cry-ing

"Cockles and mussels, a-live, a-live, oh!"

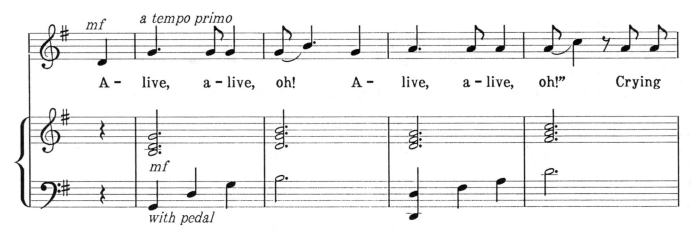

A-live, a-live, oh! A-live, a-live, oh!" Crying

"Cockles and mussels, a-live, a-live, oh!"___

I Know Where I'm Goin'

Traditional

County Antrim, Ireland
Arranged by Herbert Hughes

I know where I'm go-in', And
I know who's go-in' with me; I know who I love, but the
dear knows who I'll mar-ry!   I have stockings of

Notes about this song are on page 238.

silk, Shoes of fine green lea- ther, Combs to buckle my hair, And a

ring for eve - ry fin - ger. Some say he's bad, But

I say he's bon-ny, The fair-est of them all, My __ hand-some, win-some

John-ny. Feather-beds are soft, And

pain-ted rooms are bon-ny, But I would leave them all To

go with my love, Johnny.

cresc.

dim.

Pensively

I know where I'm go-in', And I know who's go-in' with me,

I know who I love, — But the dear knows who I'll marry!

Early One Morning

Traditional

England

Arranged by V. A. C. and J. G. P.

1. Ear- ly one morn - ing, just as the sun was
3. Re - mem-ber the vows_ that you made_ to your

ris - ing, I heard a maid_ sing in the val- ley be - low:
Ma - ry, Re - mem - ber the bow'r where you vowed to be true!

"Oh, don't de - ceive me! Oh, nev- er leave me! How could you

Notes about this song are on page 239.

use — a — poor — maid-en so?" 2. "Oh, gay is the gar- land, —
                                  4. Thus sang the poor maid- en, her

fresh are the ros - es I culled from the gar - den to
sor - row be - wail - ing, Thus sang the poor maid — in the

bind on your brow. Oh, don't de - ceive me! Oh, nev-er
val - ley be - low:

leave — me! How could you use — a — poor maid-en so?"

High Barbaree

Traditional

Sea Chantey

Arranged by V. A. C. and J. G. P.

Moderato con spirito

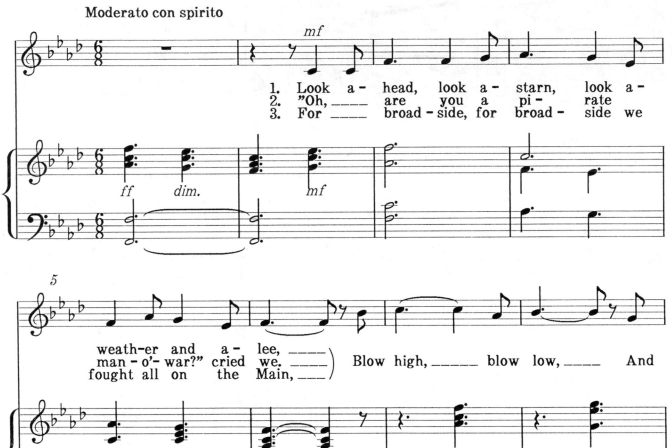

1. Look a- head, look a- starn, look a- rate
2. "Oh, _____ are you a pi- rate
3. For _____ broad- side, for broad- side we

weath-er and a- lee, _____ Blow high, _____ blow low, _____ And
man-o'- war?" cried we. _____
fought all on the Main, _____

so _____ sail- ed we. _____
"Oh, I am not a pi- rate but a
Un- til at last the fri- gate shot the

Notes about this song are on page 239.

see them all a-drown-ing as _ they tried to swim a - shore, _____ A-

sail-ing down all   on the coast of High   Bar - _ ba - ree.

The Fairy's Lullaby

Traditional

Translated by Edward Walsh

Ireland

Arranged by Alfred Moffatt

Andante tranquillo

1. Sweet babe, a gol - den   cra - dle holds thee,
2.   Rest thee, babe, for soon thy slum - bers,

Notes about this song are on page 239.

Shu-heen sho,   lu - lo - lo --   Soft   the snow-white fleece en- folds thee,
                                       Fly   at the ma - gic Koel-shee's num- bers

Shu-heen sho,   lu - lo - lo. In _   air - y bow'rs I'll watch thy sleep-ing

Shu-heen   sho,   lu - lo - lo, Where bran-chy trees to the breeze are

rit.   *pp*

sweep-ing, Shu-heen sho,   lu - lo - lo,   shu - heen   sho.

rit.

pp

Separazione

Traditional

Italy
Arranged by Giovanni Sgambati

Literal translation: Sad parting; ah, how hard it is! How great is the pain for me, the bitter pain!

Notes about this song are on page 239.

pe - na a - ma - - - ra! Do - lo - ro - -

- sa spar - ten - - - za, Ahi, quan - to è du - - -

ra! Quan - to è gran - - de per me ____ la ____

pe - na, la pe - na a - ma - - ra!

El Tecolote

Traditional

Mexico

Arranged by J. G. P.

Te-co - lo-te de Gua - dia - na,

Pa - ja-ro ma-dru-ga - dor, Te-co - lo-te de Gua - dia - na,

Pa - ja-ro ma-dru-ga - dor, Pa-ra que vue-las de no-che, Pa - ra

Literal translation: Guadiana owl,/ morning bird,/ why do you fly at night/

Notes about this song are on page 239.

when you have the day for yourself?/ Poor owl,/ you are already tired of flying.

Walk Together, Children

Traditional

Spiritual

Arranged by V. A. C. and J. G. P.

Notes about this song are on page 239.

It Was a Lover and His Lass

William Shakespeare

Thomas Morley
Edited by J. G. P.

1. It was a lov - er and his lass,
2. Be - tween the a - cres of the rye,
3. This ca - rol they be - gan that hour,
4. Then, pret - ty lov - ers take the time,

) With a

hay, and a ho, and a hay no-ni no, and a hay _____

_____ no - ni no - ni no.

That
These
How
For

Notes about this song are on page 240.

122

That' oer

123

time,   in spring - time, the

on - ly pret - ty ring - time, When birds do sing, Hay

ding-a-ding-a-ding, Hay ding-a-ding-a-ding, Hay

ding-a-ding-a-ding, Sweet lov - ers love the spring.

What If a Day

Thomas Campion?

Thomas Campion?
Arranged by J. G. P.

[Optional introduction]

1. What if a day, or a month, or a year
Crown thy de - sire with a thou - sand sweet con -
tent - ings? Can - not the chance of a night or an hour

2. Earth's but a point to the world, and a man
Is but a point to the world's com - par - ed
cen - ter; Shall then the point of a point be so vain,

Notes about this song are on page 240.

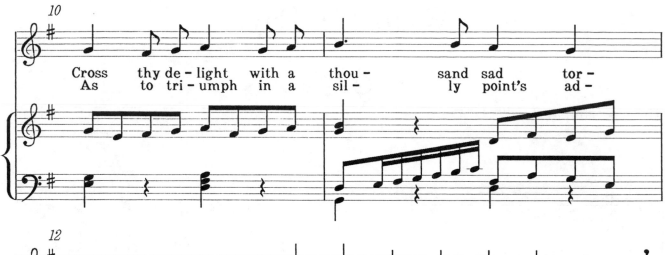

Cross thy de-light with a thou- sand sad tor-
As to tri-umph in a sil- ly point's ad-

ment- ings? For- tune, hon- or, beau-ty, youth,
ven- ture? All is haz- ard that we have,

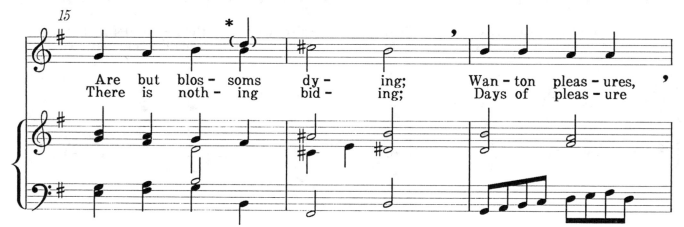

Are but blos- soms dy- ing; Wan- ton pleas-ures,
There is noth- ing bid- ing; Days of pleas-ure

dot- ing love, Are but shad- ows
are like streams Through fair mead- owsts

* Sing either b or d; both are given in early sources.

fly - ing. All our joys are but toys,
glid - ing. Weal and woe, time doth go,

I - dle thoughts de - ceiv - ing; None hath pow'r of an
Time is nev - er turn - ing; Se - cret fates guide our

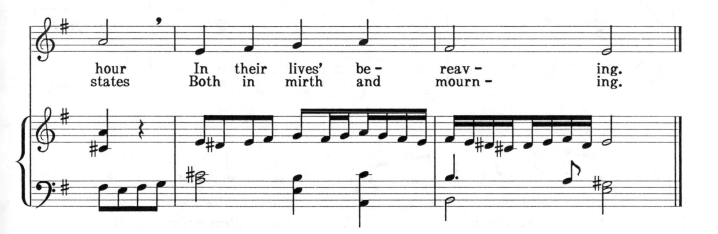

hour In their lives' be - reav - ing.
states Both in mirth and mourn - ing.

* Perform either g or g#; both are given in early sources.

When Laura Smiles

Philip Rosseter

Philip Rosseter
Edited by J. G. P.

1. When Lau- ra smiles, _____ her sight re- vives _____ both night and day. The earth and heav- en views with de- light _____ her wan- ton play,
2. Love hath no fire _____ but what he steals _____ from her bright eyes. Time hath no pow'r _____ but __ that which in _____ her pleas- ure lies,

Notes about this song are on page 241.

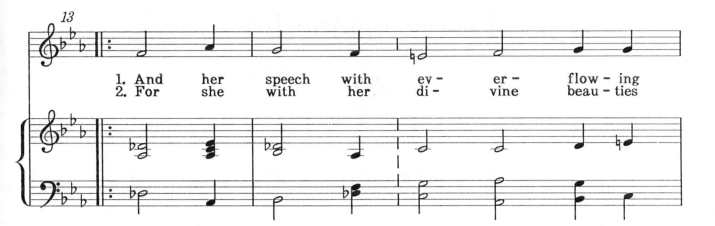

1. And her speech with ev - er - flow - ing
2. For she with her di - vine beau - ties

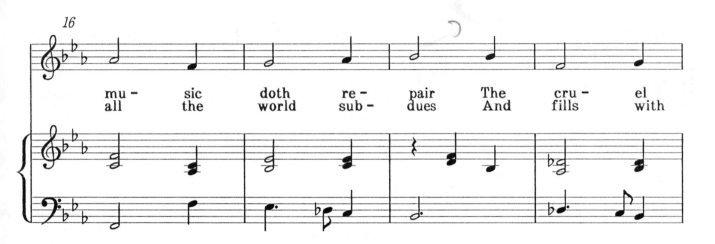

mu - sic doth re - pair The cru - el
all the world sub - dues And fills el with

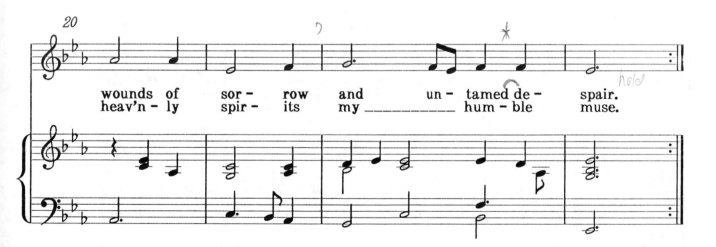

wounds of sor - row and un - tamed de - spair.
heav'n - ly spir - its my _____ hum - ble muse.

hold

Lasciatemi morire

Ottavio Rinuccini

Claudio Monteverdi
Edited by J. G. P.

La - scia - - - te - mi mo - ri - - re!

La - scia - te - mi mo - ri - re!

E che vo - le - te voi ___ che mi con - for - te

Literal translation: Let me die!/ And what do you think could comfort me/

Notes about this song are on page 241.

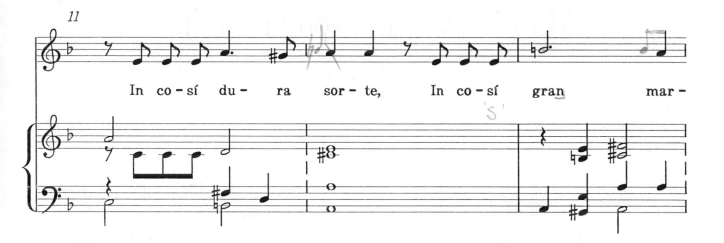

In co - sí du - ra sor - te, In co - sí gran mar -

ti - re? La - scia - - - te - mi mo - ri - re!

La - scia - te - mi mo - ri - re!

in such a hard fate,/ in such great suffering?/ Let me die!

Man Is for the Woman Made

Peter Anthony Motteux

Henry Purcell
Edited by V. A. C. and J. G. P.

Notes about this song are on page 242.

Vado ben spesso

Anonymous

Giovanni Bononcini
Edited by J. G. P.

Va - do ben spes- so can - gian-do __ lo - co,

Va - do ben spes- so can - gian-do __ lo - co,

Literal translation: I go often from place to place,/ but I never change my desire./

Notes about this song are on page 242.

Ma   non sò mai can-giar de - si - o.

Va - do ben spes - so   can-gian-do lo - co,

Ma   non   sò   mai,   ma   non sò mai,

ma _____ non sò mai can-giar de- si - o,

Ma non sò mai, ma non sò mai,
ma _____ non sò mai cangiar de- si - - o,

Fine

Sem- pre l'i-stes - so sa -

rà il mio fo - co,

Always the same will be my love.

Sem- pre l'i-stes-so sa- rà il mio fo- co, e sa- rò sem- pre l'i-

stes- so an-ch'i - o, e sa- rò sem- pre,

e sa- rò sem - - - - - - pre l'i- stes - so an-

ch'i - o, l'i- stes-so an- ch'i - o.

Da Capo al Fine

Da Capo al Fine

and I shall be the same, too.

My Lovely Celia

Anonymous
Altered by H. Lane Wilson, 1899, and by J. G. P.

George Monro
Edited by J. G. P.

Notes about this song are on page 243.

soft _____ as _ air,
oft _____ a - - rise.

No more _____ tor -
My heart's ___ en -

ment me,
chant - ed

but _____ be _ kind,
with _____ your charms;

And
O

with ___ your love ___, you'll ease _ my mind.
take ___ me, dy - ing, , to ___ your arms.

The Miller of Mansfield

R. Dodsley

Thomas Augustine Arne
Edited by J. G. P.

Allegro

1. How hap - py a state does the mil - ler pos - sess, Who
2. Tho' his hands are so daubed they're not fit to be seen, The
3. Or should he en - deav - or to heap an es - tate, In

would be no great - er nor fears to be less, On his mill and him - self he de -
hands of his bet - ters are not ve - ry clean, A __ palm more po - lite may as
this, too, he mim - ics the tools of the state, Whose aim is a - lone their own

pends for sup - port, Which is bet - ter than ser - vile - ly cring - ing at court.
dir - ti - ly deal, Gold in hand - ling will stick to the fin - gers like meal.
cof - fers to fill, As __ all his con - cerns to bring grist to his mill.

Notes about this song are on page 244.

What tho' he all dus- ty and whit- ened doth go, The
And if when a pud- ding for din- ner he lacks, He
He eats when he's hun- gry, he drinks when he's dry, And

more he's be- powd- ered, the more like a beau. A
cribs with- out scru- ple from oth- er men's sacks, In
down when he's wea- ry con- tent- ed does lie. Then

clown in his dress may be
this of right no- ble ex-
ris- es up cheer- ful to

hon- est- er far Than a
am- ples he brags, Who __
work and to sing: If so

cour- tier who struts in a
bor- row as free- ly from
hap- py's a mil- ler, then

gar- ter and star, than a
oth- er men's bags, who __
who'd be a king, if so

cour- tier who struts in his gar- ter and star.
bor- row as free- ly from oth- er men's bags.
hap- py's a mil- ler, then who'd be a king?

Nina

Anonymous

Naples, Italy (attr. to Pergolesi)

Arranged by V. A. C. and J. G. P.

Tre gior-ni son che Ni- na,, che Ni- na In
Il son- no l'as- sas- si- na,, l'as- sas- si- na, Sve-

let- to se ne sta, _____ in_ let- to_ se ne
glia- te-la per pie- tà, _____ sve- glia- te- la per pie-

stà.
tà.

E cim- ba-li, tim- pa-ni, pif- fe-ri! Sve-

Literal translation: It is now three days that Nina/ has been lying in bed./ Sleep is killing her:/ waken her, please./ Cymbals, drums, fifes./ awaken

Notes about this song are on page 244.

gliа - - te mia Ni - net - ta, Sve - glia - - te mia Ni -

net - ta, Ac - ciò non dor - ma più, _____ Ac -

ciò_ non_ dor - ma più. Sve-glia-te-mi Ni - net - ta, Ni -

net - ta, ac - - ciò ___ non_ dor - ma _ più.

my dear Nina,/ so that she will not sleep any more.

Sigh No More, Ladies

William Shakespeare

Richard J. S. Stevens
Arranged by J. L. Hatton and E. Faning

Allegretto

Sigh no more, la - dies, la - dies, sigh no more, _____
Sing no more, la - dies, la - dies, sing no more __ Of

Men were de-ceiv-ers ev - er, men were de-ceiv-ers ev - er;
dumps so __ dull and hea-vy, of dumps so __ dull and hea-vy;

One foot in sea and one _____ on shore, _____ To
The fraud of men was ev - - er so, _____ Since

Notes about this song are on page 244.

one thing con-stant nev-er,   to   one thing con-stant nev-er.
sum-mer first was lea-vy,   since   sum-mer first was lea-vy.

Then sigh not so,   but   let   them go,   And

be you blithe and bon-ny,   and   be you blithe and   bon-ny,   Con -

vert-ing   all   your sounds of woe, con- vert-ing   all   your sounds of woe To

Nel cor piu non mi sento

Giuseppe Palomba

Giovanni Paisiello
Arranged and edited by J. G. P.

Notes about this song are on page 244.

Literal translation: (1) In my heart I no longer feel/ the brightness of youth./ The cause of my torment?/ Love,
(2) I hear you, yes, I hear you,/ beautiful flower of youth!/ The cause of my torment?/

(Female) *you are guilty./ You pick on me, bite me,/ prick me, pinch me--/ what is all this?/ Pity, pity!/ Love is a certain*
(Male) *My soul, you are it./ You pick on me, bite me,/ prick me, pinch me--/ what is all this?/ Pity, pity!/ That face has*
 a certain

(Both:) something/ that makes me rave!

tà, pie- tà, pie- tà, _____ A- mo- re è un cer- to

tà, pie- tà, pie- tà, _____ Quel vi- so ha un cer- to

che, Che de- li- rar __ mi fa!

che, Che de- li- rar __ mi fa!

The solo version of "Nel cor..." ends with m. 28; it may be repeated with ornamentation. For the duet used in the opera, a female sings the first stanza, a male sings the second stanza, and after the second ending (m. 29), both singers sing the duet conclusion.

Bald wehen uns des Fruehlings Luefte

Spring Song

Anonymous

Joseph Haydn

English version by J. G. P.

Poco Adagio

Bald we-hen uns des Früh-lings Lüf-te, Bald wird der dun-kle Hain be-lebt, Es at-men schon der Kräu-ter Düf-te, In-des sich je-der Sa-me

We now can feel the spring-time stir-ring, And soon the woods will lose their gloom. We see the signs of change oc-cur-ring As plants pre-pare to grow and

Literal translation: Soon the spring breezes will blow,/ soon the dark grove will fill with life:/ plants are becoming fragrant,/ while every seed

Notes about this song are on page 245.

regt. _____
bloom. ___
Auch uns steigt Won-ne heut her-
We   too, set free from win-try

nie-   der,   Da   wir dein Na-mens-fest be- gehn;   Ver-
wea-   ther,   En - joy   the sun-ny skies a - bove.   Oh,

nimm, O Menschenfreund, die   Lie-   der,   der Schöp-fer hö-re un-ser
let us   share our joy to- geth-   er   And praise our great Cre-a-tor's

flehn,   der Schöp-fer hö-re un-ser Fleh'n.
love,   And praise our great Cre-a-tor's love.

awakens./ Joy comes down upon us, too,/ because it is your special day;/ hear, dear friend, our songs,/ and may God hear
our prayers.

Bitten

Prayer

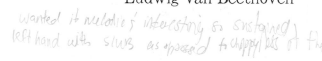

Christian Fürchtegott Gellert

Translation by V. A. C. and J. G. P.

Ludwig van Beethoven

Feierlich und mit Andacht
Solemnly and with devotion

Gott, dei - ne
O God, your

Gü - - te reicht___ so weit, So weit die Wol - ken
good - - ness reach - - es far, As far as clouds a -

Literal translation: God, your goodness reaches/ as far as the clouds./

Notes about this song are on page 245.

You crown us with your mercy/ and hurry to support us./ Lord, my fortress,, my rock, my protection,/ hear my pleading,

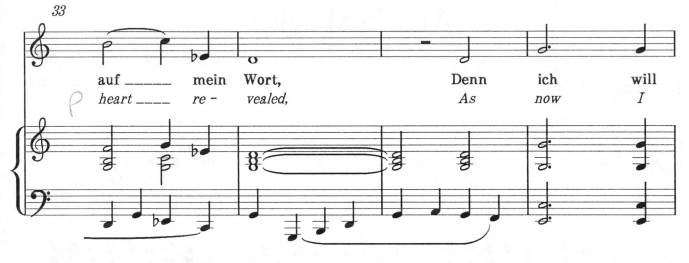

auf _____ mein Wort,   Denn   ich   will
heart _____ re - vealed,   As   now   I

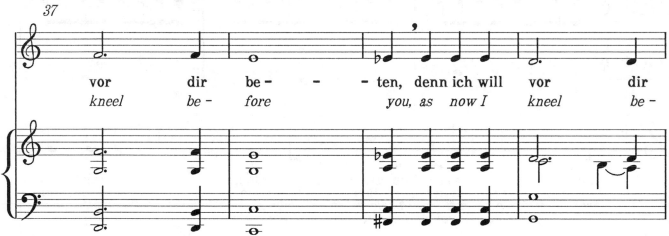

vor   dir   be - - ten, denn ich will   vor   dir
kneel   be -   fore   you, as   now I   kneel   be -

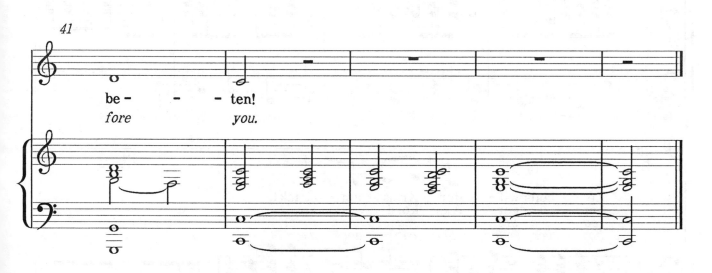

be - - ten!
fore   you.

heed my words,/   because I want to pray to you.

An die Musik

To Music

Franz von Schober
Translation by Bernard U. Taylor

Franz Schubert

Mässig *(Moderately)*

Literal translation: (1) You lovely art, in how many gray hours,/ when life's wildness entrapped me,/
(2) Often a sigh, escaped from your harp,/ a sweet, holy chord of yours,/

Translation used by permission. Notes about this song are on page 246.

Hast du mein Herz ___ zu ___ warm-er Lieb' ent-
Den Him-mel bes'- -rer Zeit- en mir_ er-
You have re-stored ___ a love, warm, rich and __
Of heav'n-ly beau-ty, of joy and peace e-

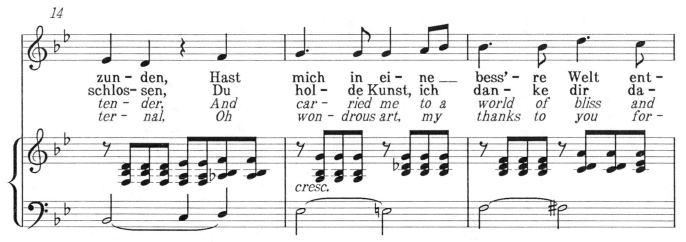

zun- den, Hast mich in ei- ne __ bess'-re Welt ent-
schlos-sen, Du hol- de Kunst, ich dan- ke dir da-
ten- der, And car- ried me to a world of bliss and
ter- nal, Oh won- drous art, my thanks to you for-

cresc.

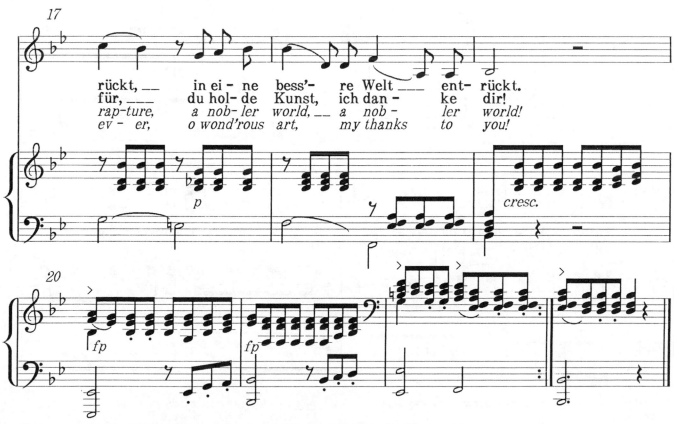

rückt, __ in ei- ne bess'- re Welt __ ent-rückt.
für, ___ du hol- de Kunst, ich dan- ke dir!
rap-ture, a nob-ler world, __ a nob- ler world!
ev- er, o wond'rous art, my thanks to you!

p

cresc.

fp   fp

(1) *have you fired my heart with warm love/ and lifted me to a better world!*
(2) *has opened a heaven of better times for me;/ you lovely art, I thank you for that!*

Wanderers Nachtlied

(Wanderer's Night Song)

Johann Wolfgang von Goethe   Franz Schubert

Literal translation: Over all the mountain-peaks/ is peace,/ in all the tree-tops/ you can hardly hear a stir:/ the birds are silent,/

Notes about this song are on page 246.

schwei-gen im _ Wal - de. War-te nur, war-te nur! Bal- de Ru-hest du
si - lent their day - song. On- ly wait, on- ly wait! Ere long You will rest,

cresc.

pp

auch. War-te nur, war-te nur! Bal- de Ru-hest du auch.
too. On- ly wait, on- ly wait! Ere long You will rest, too.

cresc.

pp   pp

are silent in the woods./ Just wait-- soon/ you will rest, too.

A Red, Red Rose

Robert Burns   Robert Schumann

Andantino   ri - tar - dan -

O my luve is like a red, __ red rose, That's new- ly sprung in

ri - tar - dan -

Notes about this song are on page 247.

June: _____ O my luve is like the mel - o-die, That's sweet- ly played in

tune. _____ As fair art thou, my bo - nie lass, So deep in luve am

I; _____ And I will love thee still, my dear, Till

a' the seas gang dry. Till a' the seas gang

Widmung
Dedication

Wolfgang Müller

Translation by J. G. P.

Robert Franz

O dan-ke nicht für die-se Lie - der, Mir ziemt es
O do not thank me for my sing - ing; I am so

dank-bar dir zu sein; Du gabst sie mir, Ich ge - be
thank-ful for these songs! From you they came; I am re-

wie - der, Was jetzt und einst und e - wig Dein.
turn - ing The gift that still to you be - longs.

Literal translation: O, do not say thanks for these songs--/ it is fitting for me to thank you!/ You gave them to me; I am giving back/ what now is and always was and will be yours./
Notes about this song are on page 247.

Yes, they were all yours:/ from the light of your dear eyes/ I read them faithfully./ Do you not recognize your own songs?

Some Folks

Stephen Foster

Stephen Foster

1. Some folks like to   sigh,
2. Some folks get grey   hairs,
3. Some folks toil and   save,

Some folks do,   some folks do;   Some folks long to   die,
Brood- ing o'er their   cares,
To buy them-selves a   grave,   But

Notes about this song are on page 247.

that's not me nor you. Long live the mer-ry, mer-ry heart That

laughs by night and day, Like the Queen of mirth, No

mat-ter what some folks say.

La Paloma

The Dove

Sebastián Yradier

Sebastián Yradier

1. Cuan- do _____
2. El di - -

_ sa- lí de la Ha- ba- na ival- ga- me Dios! Na- die _____
_ a que nos ca- se- mos ival- ga- me Dios! En la i - -

Literal translation: (Stanza 1) When I sailed from Habana, bless me,/ no one
(Stanza 2) The day we get married, bless me,/ in the

Notes about this song are on page 247.

166

me ha vis-to sa-lir ___ si no fuí yo. _____ U-
-gle-sia ca-te- dral, al-lá voy yo. _____ Des-

na _____ lin-da Gua-chi- nan-ga, a-llá voy yo,
de _____ la i-gle-sia jun-ti- tos, que sí se- ñor,

Que se _____ vi-no tras de mi, ___ que sí se-
Nos i- - -re-mos a dor-mir, ___ a-llá voy

(Stanza 1) saw me leave, except myself./ A pretty Mexico City girl I saw/ who followed me, yes sir!/
(Stanza 2) cathedral, we'll go/ from the church together, yes sir./ we will go to sleep, you bet!

(Refrain:) *If a dove comes to your window,/ treat it kindly; it is my soul./ Tell it of your love, darling,/ crown it with flowers because it is mine./ O little one, yes!/ O give me your love!/ O*

que ven-te con- mi-go, chi- ni - ta,   a don-de vi-vo   yo!

¡Ay! chi - ni-ta, que sí!   ¡Ay! que da- me tu a- mor!   ¡Ay! __

que ven-te con- mi-go, chi - ni - ta,   a don-de vi - vo   yo!

D.S. (to 2nd stanza)

come with me, darling, to where I live.

Hebe

Léon Ackermann

Ernest Chausson

Les yeux bais- sés, rou-gis- san-te et can-di- de,

Vers leur ban-quet quand Hé - bé s'a- van-çait, Les Dieux char-més ten-

daient leur cou-pe vi- de, Et de nec- tar __ l'en-fant la rem-plis-sait.

Literal translation: With eyes lowered, blushing and innocent./ Hebe approached the gods' banquet; charmed, they held out their empty cups,/ and she filled them with nectar./

Notes about this song are on page 247.

We, too, when youth passes,/ hold out our cups the same way./ What is the wine that the goddess pours?

Nous l'ig-no - rons; il en-

i - - - vre et ra - vie.

A - yant sou - ri dans sa

grâ - ce im - mor - tel - le, Hé - bé s'é - loig - - ne;

We do not know: it intoxicates and delights./ Smiling with immortal grace,,/ Hebe leaves;

we call to her in vain./ Long after, on the endless path,/ with tears, we watch the divine cup-bearer.

Ach Lieb, ich muss nun scheiden

Ah, Love, I Now Must Leave You

Copyright 1910, Oliver Ditson Company.

Felix Dahn
Translation by J. G. P.

Richard Strauss

Literal translation: Ah, love, I now must say goodbye/ and go over mountain and valley./ The alders and willows are weeping together./ They saw us so often

Notes about this song are on page 248.

12

wan - dern Zu - sam-men an Ba - ches Rand, Das Ei - ne ohn' den
walk - ing To - geth - er and hand in hand; Now one with-out the

16

An - dern geht ü - ber ih - ren Ver-stand. Die
oth - er is more than they un-der-stand. The

20

Er - len und die Wei - den vor Schmerz in Trä-nen stehn,
wil - lows and the al - - ders are weep - ing for our woe,

24

rit.

Nun den-ket, wie uns bei - den erst muss zu Herz - en
Just think what we two lov - ers must feel at part - ing

sfz   *dim.*   *p*   *cresc.*   *rit.*

walking/ together by the brook,/ that to see one without the other/ goes beyond their understanding./ The willows and
alders ard the willows/ are weeping sorrowfully./ Now think, how both of us/ must feel in our hearts.

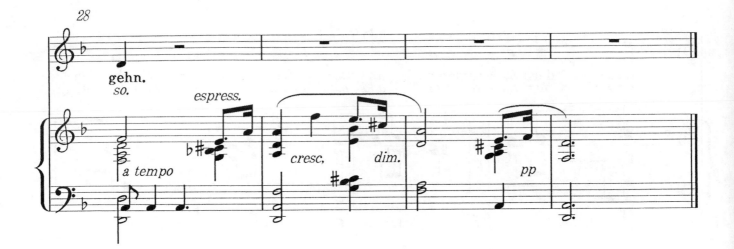

gehn.
so.

The Country of the Camisards

Robert Louis Stevenson

Sidney Homer

We trav-elled in the print of old-en wars, Yet all the land was green, _____ And love we

Notes about this song are on page 248.

found, and   peace, Where fire and war had   been.

They pass and smile, the chil-dren of   the   sword, No

more the   sword they wield;   And 0,   how deep the corn _____
(wheat)

__ A-long the bat - tle - field!

Remembrance

"The music in my heart I bore
Long after it was heard no more."
Wordsworth

Notes about this song are on page 248.

At the River

Robert R. Lowry

Robert R. Lowry
Arranged by Charles Ives

Notes about this song are on page 249.

To a Brown Girl, Dead

Countee Cullen

Margaret Bonds

Notes about this song are on page 249.

I Went to Heaven

Emily Dickinson

George Walker

Notes about this song are on page 249.

Stil-ler than the fields _____ At the first dew,

Beau- ti - ful as pic - tures No man drew.

Peo-ple like the moth, Of Mech - lin frames,

Du - ties of gos - sa- mer, And

A Christmas Carol

Anonymous, around 1500

Ned Rorem

Notes about this song are on page 249.

This
vir - gin clear Who had no peer Un - to her son did say, ___ "I ___
pray, thee, son, grant me a boon To sing by - by, ___ lul -
lay. ___ Let

Ain't Misbehavin'

Andy Razaf

Thomas Waller and Harry Brooks

Boy: Tho' it's a fick-le age   With flirt-ing all the   rage,
Girl: Your type of man is   rare,   I know you real-ly   care.

Here is one bird with self-con-trol, ___ Hap-py in-side my   cage.
That's why my con-science nev-er sleeps ___ When you're a-way some-where.

Notes about this song are on page 249.

17

I know who I love best, Thumbs down to all the rest;
Sure was a luck-y day When fate sent you my way

21

My love was giv-en, heart and soul, So it can stand the test.
And made you mine a - lone for keeps, Dit - to to all you say.

25 **Chorus**
Slowly, with expression

No one to talk with, all by my-self, No one to walk with, but
I know for cer- tain the one I love; I'm thru with flirt-in', it's

I'm hap-py on the shelf, Ain't mis-be- hav-in', I'm sav-in' my love for
just you I'm think- in' of, Ain't mis-be- hav-in', I'm sav-in' my love for

Like Jack Horn-er   in the corn-er,   Don't go no-where,

what do I care?   Your kis - ses   are worth wait - ing

for,   Be - - lieve   me.   I don't stay out late,

don't care to go, I'm home a-bout eight, just me and my ra - di - o,

Ain't mis - be - hav - in', I'm sav - in' my love for

you. you.

Love Is Here to Stay

Ira Gershwin   George Gershwin

The more I read the pa-pers The less I com-pre-hend The world and all its ca-pers And how it all will end.

Notes about this song are on page 250.

Noth-ing seems to be last- ing, But that is - n't our af - fair;

We've got some-thing per-ma-nent, I mean in the way we

care. _____ It's ve - ry clear Our love is here to

Refrain

stay; Not for a year, But ev - er and a

day. The ra-di- o and the tel-e-phone and the mov-ies that we know May just be pass-ing fan-cies, And in time may go. But, oh my dear, Our love is here to stay; To- geth- er

A Cockeyed Optimist

Oscar Hammerstein II

Richard Rodgers

Notes about this song are on page 250.

17
call me a cock-eyed op-ti-mist, Im-ma-
on-ly a cock-eyed op-ti-mist, And I
21
1
ture and in-cur-a-bly green! I have
can't get it in-to my
25
2
head. I hear the hu-man race is
29
poco rit.
fall-ing on its face And has-n't ver-y far to
poco rit.

go, _____ But ev'-ry whip-poor-will is

sell — ing me a bill, And tell — ing me it just ain't

so. _____ I could say life is just a bowl of jel — lo, _____

__ And ap — pear more in — tel — li — gent and smart, _____ But I'm

Brush Up Your Shakespeare

Cole Porter   Cole Porter

Notes about this song are on page 250.

try, So, to win their hearts, one must quote with ease Aes-chy-lus

and Eu - ri - pi - des. One must know Ho-mer and, b'lieve me, bo',

Soph- o- cles, al-so Sap-pho - ho. Un- less you know Shel-ley and

Keats and Pope, Dain- ty deb-bies will call you a dope. But the po - et

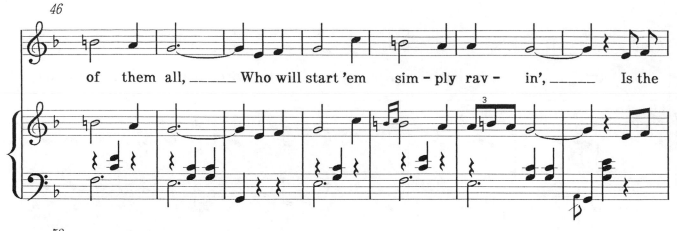

of them all, _____ Who will start 'em sim - ply rav - in', _____ Is the

po - et peo - ple call _____ "The bard of Strat-ford-on - A-von."

Brush up your Shake-speare, Start

quot-ing him now. _____ Brush up your Shake-speare,

and the wo-men you will wow.
(1.) Just de- claim a few
(2.) With the wife of the
(3.) If you can't be a

lines from *O- thel- la,*
Brit- ish Em- bessi-da
ham and do *Ham-let,*

And they'll think you're a hell-uv-a fel- la.
Try a crack out of *Troi-lus and Cressi-da.*
They will not give a damn or a damn-let.

If your blonde won't re- spond when you flat-ter 'r,
If she says she won't buy it or tike it,
Just re- cite an oc- ca- sion- al son- net,

Tell her what To - ny
Make her tike it, what's
And your lap 'll have

told Cle- o- pat-er-er.
more, *As You Like It.*
"Hon-ey" up- on ___ it.

If she fights when her clothes you are muss-ing,
If she says your be- hav- ior is hein- ous,
When your ba- by is plead-ing for pleas-ure,

What are clothes? *Much A - do A - bout Noth-ing.*
Kick her right in the *Cor - i - o - lan - us.*
Let her sam - ple your *Meas-ure for Meas-ure.*

Brush up your

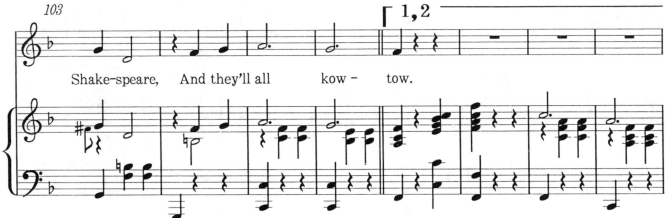

Shake-speare, And they'll all kow - tow.

tow, For-sooth, and they'll

all kow - tow, *I' faith,* and they'll all kow - tow.

Far From the Home I Love

Sheldon Harnick

Jerry Bock

How can I hope to make you un – der – stand Why I do what I do?

Why I must trav-el to a dis – tant land, Far from the home I

Notes about this song are on page 250.

25 Meno mosso – in 4

Help-less now, I stand with him, Watch-ing old-er dreams grow dim.

p

poco rit.

29 In 2

Oh, what a mel-an-cho-ly choice this is, Want-ing home,

32

want-ing him, Clos-ing my heart to ev'-ry hope but his,

35

Leav-ing the home I love.

There where my heart has set-tled

cresc.

p

long a - go,   I must go,   I must go.

Who could im - a - gine I'd be wand-'ring so   Far from the home I

In 4

love?   Yet   there with my love I'm home.

Anyone Can Whistle

Stephen Sondheim

Stephen Sondheim

An-y-one can whis-tle, that's what they say-- Eas-y.

An - y - one can whis-tle an-y old day-- Eas-y.

Notes about this song are on page 250.

It's all so sim-ple: Re-lax, let go, let

fly. So some-one tell me why can't I? _____

I can dance a tan-go, I can read Greek -- Eas-y

I can slay a dra-gon an-y old week -- Eas-y. _____

What's hard is sim-ple, What's nat-u-ral comes

hard. May-be you could show me how to let go,

low-er my guard, learn to be free. May-be if you whis-tle,

whis-tle for me. _____

He Wasn't You
She Wasn't You

Alan Jay Lerner

Burton Lane

Slowly

(Daisy)   Why   did my heart nev-er yearn be-fore?
(Edward)   Why   did each love melt a- way be-fore?

Flame af-ter flame nev-er burn be-fore?   He   was-n't you,
Heav- en a - bove turn to clay be-fore?   She   was-n't you,

Notes about this song are on page 250.

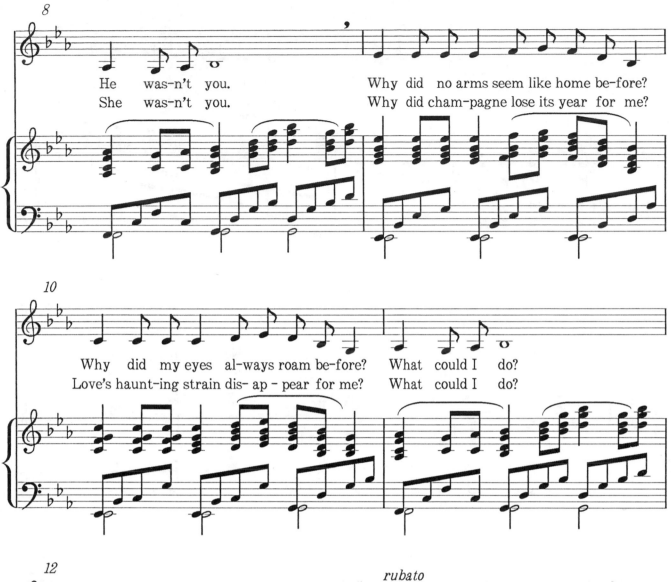

He was-n't you. / Why did no arms seem like home be-fore?
She was-n't you. / Why did cham-pagne lose its year for me?

Why did my eyes al-ways roam be-fore? / What could I do?
Love's haunt-ing strain dis-ap-pear for me? / What could I do?

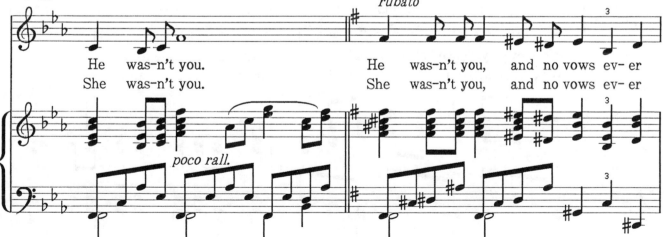

He was-n't you. / He was-n't you, and no vows ev-er
She was-n't you. / She was-n't you, and no vows ev-er

rubato

poco rall.

chained   me.   No,   he   was-n't you,   and good-byes nev-er
chained   me.   No,   she   was-n't you,   and good-byes nev-er

pained   me. _____   Now   I   know
pained   me. _____   Now   I   know

Why ev-'ry hope al- ways fad-ed so   fast: _____
Why each af- fair al- ways fad-ed so   fast: _____

On-ly with you was I born to live; On-ly to you have I love to give,
On-ly with you was I born to live; On-ly to you is the love I give

Love that for all of a life-time will
Love for as long as a life-time can

rall.　*cresc.*

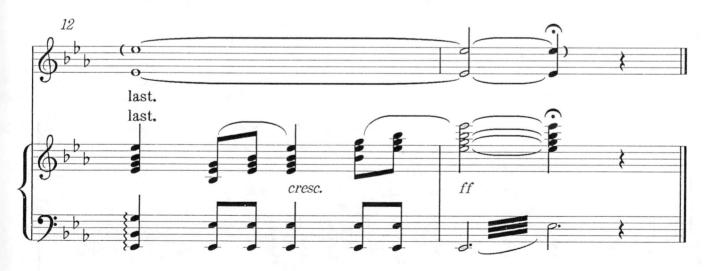

last.
last.

cresc.　*ff*

Broadway Baby

Stephen Sondheim

Stephen Sondheim

I'm just a Broad-way Ba-by,
Broad-way Ba-by,

Walk-ing off my ti-red feet,____
Slav-ing at a 5 & 10,____

Pound-ing For-ty-Sec-ond Street ____ to be in a show.____
Dream-ing of the great day when ___ I'll be in a show.____

Notes about this song are on page 250.

Say, Mis - ter Pro - du - cer,

I'm talk - - ing to you, _____ sir, _____

I don't need a lot, On - ly what I got,

Plus a tube of grease-paint and a fol - low - spot! _ I'm a

D. S. al ⊕

43 Coda

I can get to strut my stuff, ___

46

Work-ing for a nice man, Like a Zieg-feld or a Weiss-man, In a

48

great big Broad-way show! _____

What I Did for Love

Edward Kleban

Marvin Hamlisch

Notes about this song are on page 250.

And I can't re-gret ___ What I did for love, ___ what I did for

And I won't for-get ___ What I did for love, ___ what I did for

love. _____ Look, my eyes are love. _____

Gone, _____ love is nev- er

gone, _____ As we tra- vel on, _____

Love's what we'll re - mem - ber.

Kiss to - day good-bye, _____ And point me t'ward to -

mor-row. _____ Wish me luck, the same to

you. _____ Won't for-get, ___

___ can't re - gret ___ What I did _____ for

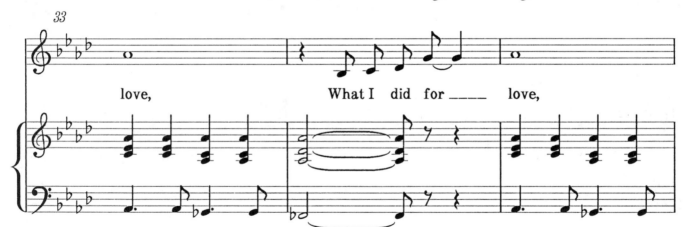

love, What I did for ____ love,

What I did for ___ love. _____

Yesterday

John Lennon and Paul McCartney

John Lennon and Paul McCartney

Moderately, with expression

Yes- ter- day _____
Sud- den- ly, _____

all my trou-bles seemed so far a- way, _____
I'm not half the man I used to be, _____

Now it looks as though they're here to stay, _____ Oh,
There's a sha- dow hang-ing o - ver me, _____ Oh,

Notes about this song are on page 251.

227

* Perform smaller notes the second time only.

Yes-ter-day, _____ love was such an eas - y game to play. _____ Now I need a place to hide a - way, ___ oh I be-lieve _____ in yes - ter - day. _____

Mm, mm, mm, mm, mm. _____

Through the Eyes of Love

Carole Bayer Sager

Marvin Hamlisch

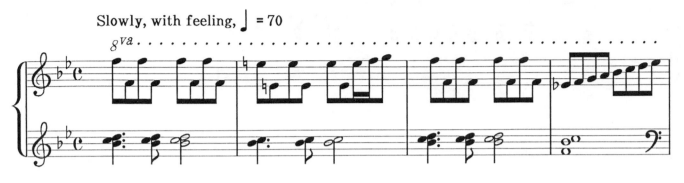

(1) Please, don't let this feel-ing end, It's ev-'ry-thing I
(2) now _____ I can take the time. I can see my
(3) Please, don't let this feel-ing end. It might not come a-

am, ev-'ry-thing I want to be. I can see what's
life as it comes up shin-ing now. Reach-ing out to
gain and I want to re-mem - ber how it feels to

Notes about this song are on page 251.

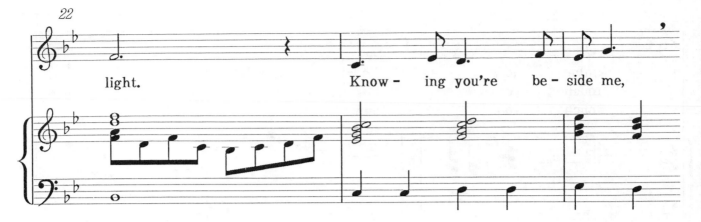

light.   Know - ing you're   be - side me,

24b   *D.S. al Coda*

I'm   all   right. _____

8va . . . .

27 ⊕ *Coda*

through   the   eyes _____ of   love.

8va . . . .

29

loco

I Just Called to Say I Love You

Stevie Wonder

Stevie Wonder

Notes about this song are on page 251.

No first of spring; _____ no song to sing,
But what it is, _____ is some-thing true
No au-tumn breeze; _____ no fal-ling leaves;
But what it is, _____ though old, so new,

1, 3

In fact, here's just a-no-ther or-di-na-ry day. _
Made up of these three words that I
Not e-ven time for birds to fly to south-ern skies.
To fill your heart like no three words

2, 4

(2.) No A-pril _ must say _ to you. _
(4.) No Li-bra _ could ev-er do. _

A Notes on the Songs

Songs for group singing

"America the Beautiful," page 96, was inspired by the view from Pike's Peak. Katherine Lee Bates, professor of English at Wellesley College, wrote the words on the morning after her climb, during a Colorado vacation in 1893. The tune by Samuel A. Ward is somewhat older, 1882.

"Auld Lang Syne," page 96, means "old long since" and refers to times past. It has become a traditional song for New Year's Eve and other times of sentimental feeling about the past. Robert Burns wrote down the words from the singing of an old man in 1791, but they are decades older. Probably the tune was old in 1783, when William Shield used it in the overture to his opera, *Rosina*. "A cup of kindness" = a friendly drink; "gie's a hand of thine" = give me your hand.

"Come, Follow!" page 97, comes from *Catch That Catch Can*, (1652). What we now call rounds were then called "catches."

"Do-Re-Mi," page 97. Set in Austria in 1938, *The Sound of Music* is based on the true story of Maria Rainer, the young governess of seven children. She married their father and became Baroness Maria von Trapp. When the family escaped Nazi persecution by emigrating, she led the children into an international concert career as the Trapp Family Singers. Mary Martin proposed putting their story on stage, and she created the leading role.

"He's Got the Whole World in His Hands," page 98. The melody of this black spiritual is given as sung by Marian Anderson on a 1962 recording. Anderson, who was the greatest concert singer of her time and the first black person ever to sing at the Metropolitan Opera, sang this spiritual at the historic rally in Washington, DC, where Dr. Martin Luther King, Jr. delivered his historic "I have a dream" speech.

"Hinay Ma Tov," page 98, is a popular Israeli melody, with words from Psalm 133. In the King James translation, the text is: "Behold, how good and how pleasant it is for brethren to dwell together in unity!" Suggestion: Divide the available singers into groups A and B. A's sing line 1 twice, then sing line 2 twice. When the A's begin line 2, B's begin line 1 and sing it twice. When B's begin line 2, A's go back to line 1 and begin again. Repeat as many times as you like, with both lines sounding together.

"Michael, Row the Boat Ashore," page 99. In the Bible, Michael and Gabriel are named as angels. "Hallelujah" = praise God (Hebrew). In spirituals, crossing the Jordan River symbolizes going to a better place, either in death or in liberation.

"Old Smokey," page 99. Some versions of this song have three-measure phrases. This version, with the end of each phrase prolonged, gives time for a leader to speak the words of the next phrase so that everyone can join in.

"The Star-Spangled Banner," page 100. Francis Scott Key, district attorney for Washington, DC, was on board a ship in Baltimore harbor, unable to land during the nighttime bombardment of Fort McHenry by the British in 1814. When morning light revealed that the fort had not surrendered, Key wrote this poem, expressing his pride. The tune is an English drinking song of the 1700s, "To Anacreon in Heaven." The United States had no official anthem until 1931, when this song was chosen. Lower notes (not part of the official anthem) are suggested here for those who are uncomfortable with the wide range of the song.

"Scarborough Fair," page 101, is a humorous song that you sing about a former sweetheart. You promise to be sweethearts again if she or he will do three tasks that, it turns out, are quite impossible.

The tune was made famous by Paul Simon and Art Garfunkel, but many other versions of "Scarborough Fair" exist. The words given here were written down in 1891 from the singing of William Moat, a fisherman of North Riding, Yorkshire, England. He sang two complete sets of words, one set appropriate for a woman and one for a man, and he followed each set with this stanza:

> And now I have answered your questions three,
> I hope you'll answer as many for me.
> I hope you'll answer as many for me,
>   And then thou shalt be a true lover of mine.

This stanza is puzzling because there are no answers to the impossible challenges. Mr. Moat's words and the melodies he sang are found in: *English Country Songs* by Lucy E. Broadwood and J. A. Fuller Maitland. London: Leadenhall Press, 1893.

"When the Saints Go Marchin' In," page 101, has gone around the world as a spiritual; I heard it sung in Italy by nuns in a religious procession. As folksong scholar Alan Lomax wrote in *The Folk Songs of North America*, "The Saints" also, "through an irony of history, has become an international hot jazz standard. The New Orleans jazz men, most of whom came from good religious homes, would never jazz up the normal spiritual, but 'The Saints' was an exception, since the Holy Rollers had already turned it into a red-hot revival tune."

Traditional songs

"Auprès de ma blonde," page 102, a lively song from northern France, celebrates the love of a happy young wife and husband. Notice that the bride's three verses all form one long sentence interrupted by the man's refrain. This alternation means that anyone can sing this song, making it widely popular.

"Cockles and Mussels," page 104. Burl Ives wrote about this song: "To the north and to the south of the port of Dublin, there are wide stretches of sand, covered by shallow water at high water. Many a 'dacint poor woman' in other days earned an honest penny by harvesting cockles and mussels, which were to be found in great numbers on these sands, and selling them on the streets of Dublin." (*Irish Songs*, 1958) Ives sang the refrain, mm 36–45, after each stanza.

"I Know Where I'm Going," page 107, a song from County Antrim in the northeast corner of Ireland, was written down and arranged by Herbert Hughes in *Irish Country Songs* in 1909. Hughes suggested that a male singer can add two notes to the first and last stanzas, singing " 'I know where I'm going,' she said, . . ." Hughes explained that in Ulster dialect "dear knows" = goodness knows. A line in stanza 3 was originally "Some say he's black," meaning sullen or ungracious. Because modern listeners will not understand this meaning, this edition changes the phrase to "Some say he's bad."

"Early One Morning," page 110. William Chappell, an authority on English folk song, first published this old song in 1840, but he did not know its source. He wrote that this was one of the songs most often sung by domestic serving girls going about their work.

"High Barbaree," page 112, refers to a battle with pirates along the coast of Barbary, the region of northern Africa between Egypt's western border and the Atlantic Ocean. Pirates ruled this part of the Mediterranean coast throughout the 1700s. "Chanteys" were sung by sailors to the rhythm of their work. The word probably comes from French *chantez*, a command to "Sing!"

"The Fairy's Lullaby," page 114. Horncastle published this song in 1844. McCarthy's *Irish Ballads* (1846) says: "A girl is supposed to be led into the fairy fort of Lisroe, where she sees her little brother, who had died about a week before, laid in a rich cradle and a young woman singing as she rocks him to sleep." This arrangement comes from *The Minstrelsy of Ireland* (1897). "Koelshee" = fairy music. "Shuheen sho, lulu lo" is a collection of soothing sounds, like the word "lullaby."

"Separazione," page 116, comes from a collection published by Guglielmo Cottrau in 1827. At that time many Italians were leaving the country to look for work in the cities or leaving Italy to come to America.

"El Tecolote," page 118, is sung to children at bedtime. "Cu-cu-ri-cu" imitates the sound of the owl. Alternation of measures in 3/4 and 6/8 meter is typically Latin-American, and the optional lower part in parallel thirds also gives a typically Mexican sound. "Tecolote de Guadiana" is a species of owl named after the Guadiana River in Spain.

"Walk Together, Children," page 120, was included in *Cabin and Plantation Songs*, 1874, as sung by students at the Hampton Institute (now Hampton University), Virginia. J. B. Towe described the origin of the song:

> This hymn was made by a company of Slaves, who were not allowed to sing or pray anywhere the old master could hear them. When he died, their old mistress looked on them with pity, and granted them the privilege of singing and praying in the cabins at night. Then they sang this hymn and shouted for joy, and gave God the honor and praise.

This story explains why mourning (for the death of the old master) is mixed with the happiness of those who have received permission to worship as they wish. "Promised Land" refers to Heaven.

This corrected edition gives the melody as it was published by two eminent black authorities on spirituals. J. Rosamond Johnson made a concert arrangement of the spiritual in 1917; he used one verse and refrain and another verse and refrain with a slightly extended ending. He described it as a "Triumphant Negro Marching Song" and suggested "tom-toms and drums" in the accompaniment.

R. Nathaniel Dett published a version for solo and choir, singing alternately. He suggested singing the verse three times, using "walk," "talk," and "sing" in succession, before going on to sing the refrain once. He supplied five full stanzas, each one with three repetitions of the verse to various words.

I do not recommend singing black dialect unless it comes naturally to you. An exception: The word "tire" has two syllables in the refrain; everyone should sing "ti-ah."

Art songs and arias

The Renaissance Period

Most of the artistic music composed during the Renaissance was choral music for church use. At the very end of the Renaissance, in Elizabethan England, new techniques in music printing and a new level of prosperity led to a flood of new songs for voice and lute. No other period has known so many good composers who wrote both poetry and music.

"It Was a Lover and His Lass," page 122, is one of the few surviving songs that may have been written especially for a Shakespearean play. Thomas Morley (1557–1602) and Shakespeare (1564–1616) were neighbors for a time in London and were undoubtedly acquainted. Morley was organist at St. Paul's Cathedral and a musician at the court of Elizabeth I.

The song occurs near the end of *As You Like It*, sung by two page boys for the amusement of a clown and his intended bride. The scene contains some clever comments on amateur singing. "Cornfield" = wheat field, "ring-time" = wedding season, and "prime" = springtime. Morley's phrase "country fools" appears in the play as "country folks."

The original music was printed for more than one person to use at a time. On a left-hand page is the music for voice and lute, but at the top of the facing page is the string bass part, printed upside down. The book was laid on a table so that the bass player read it from one side and the lutenist-singer read it from the other. Below the voice part are the symbols of a lute tablature, alphabet letters arranged along horizontal lines that represent the lute's six strings (tuned G-c-f-a-d'-g'). Each letter indicates a fret where the string should be stopped, and further symbols indicate rhythm. This system leaves no doubt exactly what notes to play, for instance, the contrasting F and F-sharp, one of the interesting features of the song.

Performance: If you imagine the comic scene with the bridal couple dancing, you will keep the tempo moving. The changing meters at m25 and m26 are not difficult; just keep the quarter-notes moving evenly, and put stresses where the words require them. Elizabethan composers often used tricks like this to keep their rhythms lively.

Accompaniment: Morley asked for lute and bass viol; guitar and cello would be next best. This edition gives exactly the notes written for lute. A pianist may want to add some notes to support the singer, especially where the lute part does not have the third of the chord.

Source: *First Booke of Ayres, or little short songs to sing and play to the lute, with the bass viole,* published by Morley in 1600 and reproduced in facsimile in *English Lute Songs*, Vol. 8, No. 33. Meter: Alla breve. Key: G major with no signature. Voice part in G clef, beginning on g1.

"What If a Day," page 125, has been known by many names; one of them, "A Friend's Advice concerning the variable changes in the world," sums up the message of the song. It is philosophical, not sad but somewhat urgent, as you warn your friend not to put too much trust in temporary happiness. A sense of mystery enters the song, especially in the final words about "secret fates."

"What If a Day" was so popular in its time that it survives in 17 hand-written and published sources dated between 1599 and 1662, including several in Dutch. The tune is still known in Holland as a folk song, "Bergen-op-Zoom," but it originated in England. A book from 1619 says that Thomas Campion (1567–1620) wrote "What If a Day," but he did not publish it in any of his books.

Source: The melody comes from *The Commonplace Book of John Lilliat* (1599), Bodleian Library, Oxford. The accompaniment is based on two lute tablatures: a book, *New Citharen Lessons* (1609) by Thomas Robinson; and a manuscript (ca. 1610), University Library, Cambridge. David Greer described the various sources in detail in *Music and Letters*, October 1962.

Both lute tablatures follow the manner used here: Each phrase is played first in block chords, then repeated in an elaborate variation. (If the accompanist prefers, the variations may be simplified or block chords played instead.) Both lute versions have a sharp before the second note of the melody, and both have the alternate higher note in m15 and m19. Neither has the raised third scale degree in m22 and m26.

"When Laura Smiles," page 128, has both words and music by Philip Rosseter (1568?–1623). We studied the poem in detail in chapter 5. Let a bright tempo swing the song along cheerfully. This lover speaks of sorrow and despair, but only to say that Laura's smile takes them away. The double-length measures, m15 and m22, are easy; just keep the quarter notes equal.

In the first edition, the page layout was like that described for "It Was a Lover and His Lass," except for being on one page with the bass part at the top, upside down.

Accompaniment: the same as for Morley's song. If a piano is used, the pianist should play the lowest notes as lightly as possible and use little or no pedal.

Source: *A Booke of Ayres* (1601), reproduced in facsimile in *English Lute Songs*, Vol. 9, No. 36. Meter: 3. Key: G major with no signature. (The third note in mm. 6 and 10 is F-natural, but probably F-sharp is assumed.) The first stanza of the text is printed under the music; three more stanzas are printed at the foot of the page. This edition uses stanzas 1 and 4. All stanzas are given in *An Anthology of Elizabethan Lute Songs, Madrigals, and Rounds*, edited by Noah Greenberg, W. H. Auden, and Chester Kallman. Some editors attribute the poem to Thomas Campion, only because Campion's songs were published in the same volume with Rosseter's.

The Baroque Period

A new musical language, the Baroque style, was born in Italy at about the same time as the English songs described above were bringing the Renaissance to a close. The Baroque style was based on the dramatic needs of opera, a new form of stage production, a play sung throughout, with music intensifying every word of the poetic text. Of several experiments that were made, the one that is usually recognized as the first opera was *Euridice* by Jacopo Peri, performed in Florence, Italy, in 1600 on the occasion of a royal wedding. The new feature of opera was an accompaniment with slow chords over which the singer had the utmost freedom to sing words expressively, not being bound to a steady rhythm. Single notes in the bass part indicated the chords, which were filled in by players who improvised on keyboard or fretted instruments. Because the bass was constantly present, we call it the *basso continuo*; and the interplay of the melody and bass parts became the identifying mark of the Baroque style.

"Lasciatemi morire," page 130, is the hopeless lament of a woman who has been left by her lover. The woman is Ariadne, a princess of Crete, who helped Theseus to escape from death in the Labyrinth. Theseus took Ariadne to the island of Naxos, where he deserted her. Her grief is expressed in a long scene, which begins with the brief section given here. (In the end Ariadne did not die. The god Dionysus married her and took her to live with the gods.)

Claudio Monteverdi (1567–1643) as a young composer published fine choral works in Renaissance style, but he adopted the new Baroque style wholeheartedly and influenced other composers as well. Because he worked for the Duke of Mantua, he probably did not see the first opera performances in Florence, but he certainly knew about them. When the Duke also wanted to see an opera, he ordered Monteverdi to write one. A *libretto*, or opera text, was obtained from Ottavio Rinuccini, who had written the texts of the Florentine operas, and Monteverdi wrote *Orfeo* in 1607. The next year he wrote *Arianna* (Ariadne's name in

Italian). The whole opera was a huge success; an eyewitness said that Ariadne's lament "moved the ladies to tears." The lament became famous; it was sung all over Italy. The rest of the opera is lost.

Monteverdi's genius appears clearly in the first measure, in the wrenching dissonance between the voice and the bass part; nothing like it had ever been heard before. Editors who published this aria in the 1800s could not understand this dissonance and avoided it by moving the bass part down at the same time as the voice moves up. The harmonic puzzle is resolved here by using the voice leading that Monteverdi himself used in a choral version of the Lament.

Performance: Know what each single word means, and then put yourself into the frame of mind of a person who is still in love but has been betrayed. Let the first note swell to the dramatic second note, but get all of your expression through the vowels rather than the consonants (this is Italian, not English). Strong consonants begin the word "gran"; roll the r vigorously.

Accompaniment: The instrumentation is lost but may have consisted of chord-playing instruments (lute, harp, or harpsichord) and a string bass.

Source: Monteverdi's autograph is lost. This edition is based on manuscript Mus. G239, owned by the Biblioteca Estense, Modena, Italy. For voice (soprano clef, starting on a1) and unfigured continuo. A manuscript in the handwriting of composer Luigi Rossi, British Library Add. 30491, is reproduced in *New Grove's Dictionary of Music and Musicians*. The harmonization in this edition is based on Monteverdi's madrigal version for five voices, published in 1614. Bibliography: "Monteverdi's 'Lamento d'Arianna'" by J. A. Westrup, *Music Review, Vol. I, 1940.*

"Man Is for the Woman Made," page 132, is a lively comic song by Henry Purcell (1659–1695), the greatest English composer. His opera *Dido and Aeneas* is still performed often, but he wrote songs for many plays that are no longer done. This song was sung in Thomas Scott's comedy *The Mock Marriage*, 1695. Peter Anthony Motteux, a music journalist and a friend of Purcell's, wrote the words.

Accompaniment: In the Baroque era harpsichord and bass viol were normally used; the bass part is the same as that of the piano part. Use no pedal; let the chords be detached when appropriate. The chords have been filled in by the editor; feel free to change them as you like.

No primary source is available, but the first measures are given in Zimmermann's catalog of Purcell's works. For voice (treble clef, starting on c2) and continuo. Key: C. Meter: alla breve. Text: *Wit and Mirth, or Pills to Purge Melancholy* (1720), Vol. III. Stanza 3, line 4, originally read "Whore, bawd or harridan. . . ."

"Vado ben spesso," page 134, "I'm always on the go, but I never forget whom I love." This jaunty tune could symbolize the whole life of Giovanni Bononcini (1670–1747), who started life anew several times in major cities. Born in Modena, Italy, he was George Frideric Handel's chief competitor for awhile in London, but he ended his career in Vienna.

"Vado ben spesso" is a good example from which to learn several terms that come up often in the history of music. We call it an *aria* (air) mainly because that is the Italian word most used for accompanied songs. It does not come from an *opera*, which is staged in a theater, nor from an *oratorio*, which is performed without staging in a church or a concert hall. It comes from a *solo cantata*, a piece meant to be sung by one singer at home, in a voice studio, or at the home of a wealthy person who can afford to hire professional musicians to entertain. "Vado ben spesso" is the first of three arias in the cantata.

This aria is longer than it looks. At the end of m46, you are instructed to go back to the beginning and start over *da capo*, "from the top." A *da capo aria* saves time for a busy composer, but audiences also liked operas made up of one da capo aria after another. Why? First, a good tune is worth hearing twice. Also, a repetition gives the singer a chance to show off by adding ornaments to the melody, in somewhat the same way as a jazz player improvises on a popular song. A quick tune like this one does not need many ornaments, but some are suggested here in small notes; try them out and then feel free to make up your own.

Accompaniment: the same as for the preceding song.

Source: British Library Additional Ms. 14,211 and Milano Conservatory Ms. Noseda C-65-7. The British manuscript gives the higher version of m27; the Milano manuscript gives the lower version. For voice (soprano clef) and continuo. Key: D. Meter: alla breve.

Franz Liszt quoted "Vado ben spesso" in "Annés de Pèlerinage," a set of piano pieces. He and others in the 1800s believed wrongly that the composer was Salvator Rosa, a famous painter.

"My Lovely Celia," page 138, is typical of popular songs in London during Handel's time. While little is known about George Monro (1680–1731), his well-liked song was reprinted several times during the 1700s.

There are two versions of the anonymous poem. The original version compared Celia to the gods of Greece. Here are two stanzas of the original five; you may sing them if you prefer. "Fresh alarms" = "new calls to battle."

> My goddess Celia, heav'nly fair,
> As lilies sweet, so soft as air;
> Let loose thy tresses, spread thy charms,
> And to my love give fresh alarms.
>
> O let me gaze on those bright eyes,
> Tho' sacred lightning from 'em flies:
> Thou art all over endless charms!
> O take me, dying, to thy arms.

H. Lane Wilson, probably feeling that the original text, containing the word "goddess," was unacceptable, wrote "My Lovely Celia," which has become well known. I have adjusted Lane's words to remove extra syllables from lines 3 and 4.

Performance: Your beloved's favorite dance is the minuet, so you sing to the smooth, stately rhythms of that dance. When you sing her name, you add an ornament to the note to make it special. The printed sign is "tr," meaning trill, but a grace-note or any other ornament will do as well. For the poetic meter "heav'n" is contracted into one syllable, but you may pronounce the syllable -ven on the fourth 8th-note to make the word clearer.

You have opportunities to carry one syllable over as many as four notes, singing as smoothly as you can. Also enjoy your chance to soar up without accompaniment on the word "more." A singer of the 1700s would certainly put a trill on the half-note in m19, beginning one note above the printed note.

Accompaniment: The introduction is not part of the original song, so you may choose not to play it. The style is the same as for Purcell's "Man Is for the Woman Made."

Source: *Musical Miscellany*, Vol. IV, pp. 124–25. London: Watts, 1730. Copy in the Library of Congress, Washington, DC. For voice (treble clef, starting on d2) and continuo. Key: G. Meter: 3/4. Heading: "Set by Mr. G. MONRO," which implies that some other person wrote the poem. Stanza 1 printed with the notes, stanzas 2–5 on the opposite page.

"The Miller of Mansfield," page 140, is proud of his mill, which grinds flour for a whole village and provides a good livelihood. If sometimes he cheats customers, he is no worse than cheaters in government, he surmises. He would not trade places with city folks, nor even with the king himself. Thomas Augustine Arne (1710–1778) wrote this song for a play, *The King and the Miller of Mansfield*, in 1737. "Beau" = an overdressed, powdered man; "garter and star" = decorations worn by nobility; "tools of the state" = persons who serve the government.

Performance: This is a "patter song," one which makes its point with rapid, clear, witty delivery of the words. Notice the holds, *fermatas*, in m18, m22, and m24. They need not be very long, only long enough to interrupt the otherwise steady tempo.

Accompaniment: The introduction is not part of the original song; you may choose not to play it. The repeated 8th's in the bass symbolize the noisiness of the miller's trade; play them, but with no pedal.

Source: "The Miller of Mansfield" in two different printings, dated 1771 and 1785, owned by the University of California at Los Angeles. Both are printed from the same plate, with "Allegro" added in the later edition. For voice (treble clef, starting on d1) and continuo. Key: G. First stanza printed with the notes, the others below.

"Nina," page 142, is a beautiful melody, surrounded by mystery. Why has Nina slept for three days? Is she dead? If so, what good will fifes and cymbals do?

Another question: Who wrote this song? Various sources name Giovanni Battista Pergolesi (1710–1736), but his brilliant talent and early death led to other persons putting his name onto many pieces that were not his. "Nina" is certainly not in any of his operas. Musicologist Frank Walker reviewed the evidence (see his article in the *Musical Times*, 1949) that the song originated in Naples and was brought to England in 1749 by an Italian opera troupe led by Vincenzo Ciampi, but that it was not composed by Ciampi.

Source: No primary source is available. This edition draws some features from F. Gevaert's *Le Chant Classique*, which was based on a London publication of 1749.

The Classical Period

As the Classical style developed in the works of J. S. Bach's sons and the works of Haydn, composers adopted the piano as a favorite instrument. There was finally a single instrument capable of providing strong and expressive partnership for even the finest singer. The Baroque custom of improvising accompaniments over a *basso continuo* died out in favor of fully written out accompaniments, either for keyboard or for orchestra.

"Sigh No More, Ladies," page 144, comes from Shakespeare's *Much Ado About Nothing*, Act II:3. Richard John Samuel Stevens (1757–1837) composed it as a *glee*, a song for several voices; but it has been sung as a solo in many productions of the play.

Source: *Songs of England*, edited by J. L. Hatton and Eaton Faning, London, no date.

'Nel cor più non mi sento," page 146, expresses a temporary case of lovesickness felt by a young woman, Rachelina, who is usually very lively. Her wooer, Coloandro, repeats her song with slightly different words, and then their voices join in a gentle complaint about this love that is causing them so much trouble.

Rachelina is the heroine of *La Molinara* (the mill owner's daughter), a comic opera written in 1788 by Giovanni Paisiello. Her aria was a concert favorite of many great sopranos, but it is only the first part of the duet. In the comic scene that follows, Coloandro goes into hiding; Rachelina sings her song again; and another man, also in love with her, shows up and joins in her song to make it a duet again.

Users of this book have asked for examples of ways to add ornaments to a melody. That is the purpose of the second vocal line, which gives my suggestions of ornaments (not Paisiello's). Try them out, choose which ones you like, and feel free to invent others, perhaps adding higher or lower notes if they are in your comfortable range.

This arrangement can be done several ways: (1) as a female solo, m1–m28, with or without the postlude, m41–m44; (2) as a female solo, singing the aria twice and varying it the second time; (3) as a male solo, singing the second text once or twice, the same as for a female; (4) the original version, with the repeat sung by the male and continuing to the duet portion in m29 to the end. Either singer may use any of the ornaments; it is not intended that the plain version is for the female and the ornamented version is for the male singer.

Source: *Antologia Classica Musicale*, Anno IV, no. 4 (1845), Milano: G. Ricordi. Full score, Florence: A. Rocchi, 1962. For soprano, tenor, and small orchestra. Original key: G. Beethoven wrote a set of piano variations on this aria.

"Bald wehen uns des Frühlings Düfte," page 151, was written by the great Austrian composer, Franz Joseph Haydn (1732–1809). Although he was 34 years older than Mozart, they admired each other's music and were good friends. Haydn's music embodies the musical style that we call Classical, that is admired for its clarity and balance.

Performance: A sense of joy and well-being fills this song about spring; the tempo is calm rather than lively. Be sure that the eighth-notes are even and equal in length. When eighths, each one-half beat long, are sung against triplets, each one third beat long, the second eighth fits exactly between the second and third triplets.

The small note in m16 is a *short appoggiatura*. Its small size does not mean it is unimportant; on the contrary, it is printed small because it is not part of the chord in the accompaniment, but that is the very fact that makes it expressive. Sing it on the beat as the first and strongest of four sixteenths.

Accompaniment: Haydn's piano was smaller than ours; the sound was lighter and clearer. Play lightly, using a more detached touch than you would use for Romantic music. In m33 and m34 notice Haydn's markings, which emphasize the falling patterns in alternating hands.

Source: *Joseph Haydn Werke*, Series 29:1, edited by Jens Peter Larsen, Muenchen: Henle, 1960. Original key: G. Of the second stanza, only one word survives. The song has no title; it is known by its first words.

"Bitten," page 153, shows us how one of the greatest composers of all time could write with simplicity. Ludwig van Beethoven (1770–1827) composed it in 1803, the same year as his Symphony No. 3, the magnificent "Eroica."

Beethoven probably meant his "Six Songs of Gellert" to be sung at home. German sacred songs were not used in the Roman Catholic churches of Austria, and there were still not many public concerts that featured songs. The poems, written by Christian Fuerchtegott Gellert (1715–1769), were widely known and had been set to music earlier by C. P. E. Bach, one of the musical sons of the great J. S. Bach.

Performance: Beethoven loved singers and singing, but he demanded the utmost of all performers. Even this brief song has one strenuous passage, mm27–32, where the voice stays on one pitch in the upper part of the voice. Be sure to breathe often enough, even at every comma, to stay physically free. Notice that m33 is suddenly soft after a long crescendo; Beethoven liked this effect and used it also in m15 and m36.

Accompaniment: Beethoven's own piano playing was much more legato than the playing of his predecessors, including Mozart. Notice how often Beethoven used slurs in the left hand, indicating that the bass should sound melodic and interesting.

Source: *Sechs Lieder von Gellert*, Opus 48, no. 1. (1803) Key: E. Tempo marking: "Feierlich und mit Andacht."

The Romantic Period

The 1800s, which began with the tumult of the Napoleonic Wars, brought radical changes into the lives of Europeans. The breakdown of old monarchies led to rebelliousness among students and intellectuals. Individual freedoms took on new importance, and individual emotions became the focus of a new artistic movement, Romanticism. Workers left the farms to work in factories, just when scholars were beginning to look seriously at folk traditions. There was a great poverty (think of Dickens's *A Christmas Carol*) and pervasive social injustice. At the same time, industrialization brought new wealth to many people; no parlor was well furnished without a piano.

"An die Musik," page 156, glows with happiness as it expresses thanks to music, which was Schubert's whole life. Like Beethoven, Schubert supported himself as a composer, but he did not have the advantage of Beethoven's fame as a piano virtuoso. He lived in poverty, often supported by his friends, until his early death.

No friend did more for young Schubert, jobless at age 20, than Franz von Schober (1796–1882), the poet of this song. After Schubert quit teaching at his father's school, Schober gave him food and lodging, opera tickets and music paper, and introduced him to a famous singer named Vogl, who made Schubert's songs known in the musical circles of Vienna.

Schubert's works are known by their numbers in the chronological catalog compiled by Otto Erich Deutsch. This song is D.547, which means that it is estimated to be Schubert's 547th work.

Performance: Many singers take this song too slowly and with a melancholy attitude; remember that it was written by two young men, whose "better world" lay in their dreams for the future. The tempo marking is "moderate," but the meter signature shows that there are only two beats to a measure, so the tempo moves along cheerfully. Practice the high notes in m13 and m16 carefully to keep them in tempo. While you sing, listen to the wonderful, melodic bass part in the pianist's left hand; think of your melody as a duet with the bass melody.

The original notation used two unusual appoggiaturas, which are shown in this edition not as they were written but as they should be sung. The first note of m5 was originally a small 8th-note slurred to a normal dotted quarter. The first note of m17 was a small quarter slurred to a normal half.

Accompaniment: Throughout the song, the left hand is more important than the right; notice the careful articulation markings that Schubert provided. Only in mm19–23 does the right hand provide a contrast to the bass; the accents in these measures probably imply a slight lingering on the dissonant, accented chords.

Source: Du holde Kunst, D.547 (March 1817). Key: D. Tempo: Mässig.

"Wanderers Nachtlied," page 158, is one of the most loved poems in German literature. It was first written in 1780 on the wall of a mountain cabin in Thuringia (now in East Germany) by Johann Wolfgang von Goethe (1749–1832), the author of "Faust" and beyond question the greatest German poet.

Franz Peter Schubert (1797–1828) learned the Classical style from singing as a boy soprano in the choir of the Imperial Chapel and from composition lessons with Antonio Salieri. Poetry led him to Romanticism, which emphasized personal feelings and love of nature, two qualities expressed in this song.

Performance: Quietness is all around, says the poem, and the music adds a sense of wonderment to the scene. You, too, will rest, says the poem, and the music adds a sense of deep satisfaction. The dynamic level is soft throughout, swelling a little at the climaxes in m10 and m12. Be sure, however, to use enough tone to be heard clearly and to have a good quality.

Source: Wanderers Nachtlied, D. 768. Key: Bb. Tempo: Langsam.

"A Red, Red Rose," page 159, is a simple love song with lyrics written by Robert Burns (1759–1796). The Romantics honored Burns as a genuine poet of the people; his poems were translated and widely read in Germany. Robert Schumann (1810–1856) wrote the melody in March 1840, six months before his marriage to Clara Wieck (the story of that marriage makes good reading). The original Scots words fit Schumann's music with slight changes. "A' the seas gang . . ." = all the seas go.

Source: *Fünf Lieder und Gesänge*, Opus 27, no. 2. Original key: A.

"Widmung," page 162, takes us to the heart of Romanticism, the artistic movement that put the expression of personal emotions ahead of every other consideration. Robert Franz (1815–1892) lived a quiet life and favored serenity in music as well, but his songs are both sincere and original.

Source: *Lieder*, Opus 14, no. 1.

"Some Folks," page 164, expresses an unbeatable determination to be happy. Stephen Collins Foster (Pittsburgh, Pennsylvania, 1826—New York City, 1864) needed this determination to make his way as a song writer. His earlier songs, written for minstrel shows, are marred by racial stereotypes; but later Foster abandoned Negro dialect and broadened his subject matter. His 200 songs have been published in many kinds of arrangements, none of which are as clear, tasteful, and correct as Foster's original versions.

Source: "Some Folks," New York, Firth & Pond, 1855.

"La Paloma," page 166, has an international origin. The Spanish song writer Sebastiàn Yradier (1809–1865) lived for awhile in Havana, Cuba, and used a Cuban rhythm, *habanera*, in his songs (Bizet used one of them without permission in his opera *Carmen*.). Yradier wrote "La Paloma" while on a visit to Mexico. It was first sung publicly in 1863 by Concha Mendez, performing in the Teatro Nacional in Mexico City, and it spread around the world as a famous Mexican song.

If you want to perform "La Paloma" as a duet, simply use the two parts played by the piano, right hand. Mexican popular songs are often done as duets, mainly in parallel thirds.

Source: No primary source is available. The Spanish text and historical background come from *Die Volksmusik der Kreolen Amerikas* (Berlin, 1911) by Albert Friedenthal, who gathered his information during travels in Latin America, 1882–1901. He recommended a tempo of MM76 to the quarter. He said that the first edition was full of errors. He gave a postlude 16m long (four repetitions of the pattern in mm58–61), which may be a later addition to the song; it has a satirical dialect text about the Austrian administration of Mexico that has no interest now.

"Hébé," page 170, was the goddess of youth in Greek mythology. Her cup of ambrosia and nectar kept the gods forever young. In this song, you think about youth slipping away (one need not be old to feel this), and you ask what is the magic drink that could keep us all young. There is no answer because Hebe, smiling, walks away.

Ernest Chausson (1855–1899), who was a student of Massenet and a close friend of Debussy, composed this song in an ancient Greek scale called the Phrygian mode, which we can hear by playing the white keys on the piano from d to d. (In the more familiar system of church modes this scale is called "Dorian.")

Source: "Hébé," Opus 2:6. Paris: J. Hamelle, no date. Original key: D minor with no flat.

"Ach Lieb, ich muss nun scheiden," page 174, takes up the eternal story of lovers
parting with the poetic simplicity and directness of German folk song.
Richard Strauss (1864–1949) began his song simply (it comes from a collection entitled "Simple Melodies"), but he heightened the emotion at the
end by writing wide leaps for the voice and by breaking the final phrase
into small fragments. Strauss, who came from Munich and was not related
to the waltz composers from Vienna, wrote extremely modern harmonies
for his time. Strauss went on to write tone poems for orchestra and large
operas with phenomenally difficult singing roles.
Source: *Schlichte Weisen*, Opus 21:3. (1888)

"The Country of the Camisards," page 176, tells the story of a visit to a historic
battlefield. It could be any battlefield, such as Gettysburg, but this particular one is in France, where Huguenots (Protestants) rose up against their
Catholic neighbors in 1702. The bloody rebellion now seems remote and
the place is peaceful.

The Scottish poet Robert Louis Stevenson suffered from tuberculosis and
traveled far and wide in search of a healthful climate. His travels led to writing
the adventure classic "Treasure Island." Sidney Homer (Boston, 1864—Winter
Park, Fl. 1953) was born in the same year as Richard Strauss and studied in
Munich. This song is dedicated to his wife, who was an internationally famous
contralto, Louise Homer.

Source: "The Country of the Camisards," Opus 15:5 (1904). Poem from *Un-
derwoods*. Original key: Db major.

The Modern Period

Around 1900 many musicians believed that such composers as Richard Strauss
had stretched conventional ways of composing to the breaking point and that
completely new ways had to be found. Charles Ives was one of the searchers,
but he worked alone, unknown to other musicians. Igor Stravinsky, Paul Hin-
demith, and Béla Bartók were among the international musicians who found
new paths and influenced the new music of the Twentieth Century.

"Remembrance," page 178, awakens a sense of mystery and nostalgia.

Charles Edward Ives (Danbury, Connecticut, 1874—New York City 1954)
played the organ in several churches from his teen years on. He studied music
at Yale, where he wrote a symphony and a string quartet. Ives went into the life
insurance field, where he became wealthy, while he wrote music outside of office
hours. Encouraged by his wife, Harmony, Ives made remarkable musical inno-
vations, including use of several keys at once and novel ways of forming chords.
His stressful life led to a heart attack in 1918. During recuperation Ives "cleaned
house" by making final copies of music written earlier, and he published *114
Songs* at his own expense in 1922. He lived in retirement for long enough to see
a growing acceptance of his music, which is now played often by major symphony orchestras.

Why are the chords in the accompaniment so strange? Ives knew that there
are beautiful sounds that lie beyond the realm of conventional major and minor
chords, just as there are ideas that lie beyond our rational understanding. Ives's
music often suggests ideas and feelings that are beyond our ability to know ra-
tionally or to put into words.

The words of the song refer to Ives's father, George Ives, who was a band-
master in the Civil War, and who influenced his son to be self-reliant and to
explore new sounds. The accompaniment uses chords built of open fifths stacked
on top of each other and other chords that spread over a wide range and contain
notes from several keys. Ives suggested a melodic instrument for the top line,
or it can be played on the piano.

Source: "Remembrance" (1921), from *114 Songs*. Original Key: no signature, voice begins on b1. A note in *114 Songs* says: "Where no author is indicated, the words are by Harmony Twichell Ives or her husband," who is, of course, Ives himself. Ives used three staves for the piano part, keeping one staff for the legato upper voice, mm. 3–7.

"At the River," page 179, is based on a beloved Baptist gospel song by Robert R. Lowry (1826–1899), who wrote both the tune and the text. The imagery comes from visions of the afterlife found in the Book of Revelations.

Please read about Charles Ives in the notes about "Remembrance." Ives often borrowed from well-known hymns because he respected people's feelings about them. "At the River" uses some phrases of Lowry's gospel song but floats the melody over chords that contain many notes from other keys with an unearthly effect. Ives departs from Lowry's melody in mm11–13 and again from m20 to the end in order to have more freedom to suggest "the throne of God" and to make clear that the end of the song is still an unanswered question. Ives himself added the note: "The piano part must not be played heavily."

Source: "At the River," (1916), based on *Sonata No. 4, Children's Day at the Camp Meeting,* for violin and piano (1914–1915). Published in *114 Songs*.

"To a Brown Girl, Dead," page 181, presents a poignant picture of Harlem life. We do not know how the girl died, only that her mother has sacrificed to make her pretty. Countee Cullen (1903–1946) was a lyric poet, a leader of the Harlem Renaissance. The poem comes from his book *Color*, 1925. Margaret Bonds (Chicago 1913—Los Angeles 1972) was a versatile musician and a prolific composer who collaborated with Langston Hughes on stage productions.

"I Went to Heaven," page 184, is a humorous song on verses by one of America's great poets, Emily Dickinson (1830–1886). The lightness of her imagery is caught by the music of Dr. George Walker (b. Washington, DC, 1922), Distinguished Professor of Music at Rutgers University. His accomplishments have been recognized by grants from the Guggenheim, Rockefeller, and Koussevitzky Foundations.

"Lathed" = built of or covered with lath, narrow strips of wood used to support plaster (in this case the lath is not wood, but feathery down). "Mechlin" = Belgian lace, "gossamer" = sheer fabric, "eider" = eiderdown, soft feathers from an eider duck.

The piano part skips quickly from one register to another and contains much silence. The voice part is in a major key; it could be given a simple harmonization as a help during the learning stages. Original key: G.

"A Christmas Carol," page 187, uses an unusual scale, Myxolydian mode, which is like a major scale but has a lowered seventh degree. The *coda*, mm32–36, goes into minor, but the last chord is major. Ned Rorem (b. Philadelphia 1923) won the 1976 Pulitzer Prize for music. His songs have become standard concert repertoire. Original key: D Mixolydian with no signature.

Songs from Broadway musicals

"Ain't Misbehavin'," page 190, written for *Hot Chocolates* (1929), remained so well-known over the years that it became the title song of a review devoted to the music of Thomas "Fats" Waller; *Ain't Misbehavin'* opened on May 9, 1978, and ran for 1,604 performances. Many stars have sung "Ain't Misbehavin'" in many different ways, but the original tempo was "slowly." Instead of singing the 8th-notes evenly, some performers "swing" them, making the onbeat 8th-notes about twice as long as the offbeat ones. The effect sounds as if the song were written in 12/8 time. Source: original edition, piano score by Harold Potter.

"Love Is Here to Stay," page 194, from *The Goldwyn Follies* (1938), is one of many song classics by the Gershwin brothers. The original orchestrations of most early musicals have been lost because no one imagined that future generations would want them. Publishers of sheet music tried to reach a broad market of musical amateurs by transposing the songs into keys that avoid unusually high or low notes and by doubling every melody note in the piano part, even though this often does not sound good. Unfortunately, the sheet music version is all we have of most Gershwin songs.

"A Cockeyed Optimist," page 198, from *South Pacific* (1949, 1,925 performances) occurs in the first scene, when Ensign Nellie Forbush, a U.S. Navy nurse in World War II, expresses her philosophy of life to a French civilian, Emile DeBecque. Mary Martin created the role of Nellie. Notice some unusual lines: "When the sky is . . . canary yellow"; "But every whippoorwill is selling me a bill . . ." (a play on "sold a bill of goods"); ". . . life is just a bowl of jello . . ." (a play on "life is just a bowl of cherries"). Nellie seems to have a flair for unusual combinations of ordinary words! The musical is based on James Michener's *Tales of the South Pacific*. Original key: F.

"Brush Up Your Shakespeare," page 202, from *Kiss Me, Kate* (1948, 1,077 performances), is sung by two gangsters, who are caught up in the spirit of an acting company that is performing *The Taming of the Shrew*. The two leads in the play quarrel as furiously offstage as onstage; the male lead stays in the production only because he owes a large gambling debt that the gangsters have come to collect. Cole Porter's sophisticated wit comes into full play. "Tony" = Antony; "kowtow" = bow to the ground; "forsooth," "I' faith" (short for "in faith") = mild Shakespearean oaths. Original key: F.

"Far From the Home I Love," page 207, from *Fiddler on the Roof* (1964, 3,242 performances), is sung by Hodel, the second daughter of Tevye, a milkman. The scene is a Jewish village in Czarist Russia around 1905. Hodel is leaving home to follow Perchik, a rebellious student who has been arrested and sent into exile in Siberia. The musical is based on stories by Sholom Aleichem. Original key: C minor.

"Anyone Can Whistle," page 211, is the title song of *Anyone Can Whistle* (1964, 9 performances). It has been revived as part of various reviews devoted to the music of Stephen Sondheim. Original key: A minor.

"He Wasn't You" or "She Wasn't You", page 214, from *On a Clear Day You Can See Forever* (1965, 280 performances) has two texts. The first is sung by Daisy Gamble, a person who recalls an earlier life when under hypnosis, and the second by Edward Moncrief, the lover she remembers from the 1700s. In the musical score Daisy (first sung by Barbara Harris) sings the song in the low belt key of Eb; Edward sings it in the high baritone key of Ab.

"Broadway Baby," page 218, from *Follies* (1971, 522 performances), shows Sondheim's skill in writing a song that deliberately imitates the hits of the 1930s. Dmitri Weissmann (m46) is a fictitious producer modeled after Florenz Ziegfeld, who produced reviews called "follies" (see the Gershwin song above). The song is sung by Hattie Walker, a woman in her seventies re-creating one of the great songs of her past. Original key: G.

"What I Did for Love," page 223, from *A Chorus Line* (1975, and still running as this is written) is sung by Diana Morales, who is auditioning to be in the chorus of a musical. When one of the dancers injures himself, perhaps ending his career, the director asks the other auditioners how they would feel if their careers ended suddenly. Morales (first sung by Priscilla Lopez) answers with this song about her love of dancing. Original key: Ab.

Popular Songs and Songs from Motion Pictures

"Yesterday," page 227, comes from the Beatles album *Help!* (1965). Although John Lennon's name appears by contractual agreement, Paul McCartney actually wrote both lyrics and music together in one sitting. George Martin's arrangement of the accompaniment used guitar and string quartet, an innovation for pop music. Original key: F.

"Through the Eyes of Love," page 230, was sung by Melissa Manchester for the motion picture *Ice Castles*. Original key: Bb.

"I Just Called to Say I Love You," page 233, was sung by Stevie Wonder for the motion picture "The Woman in Red." Original key: Db. After verse 4, Wonder suddenly shifts the key up one half-step (third beat of m23), which a pianist can easily do by imagining the key signature changed (Bb to B, or Db to D). Wonder sings the last note of the song a third lower than written, saving the high note for a later repetition of the song.

B The International Phonetic Alphabet

These are the symbols of the International Phonetic Alphabet (IPA) as they are used in singing English. They are given in this order: vowels, semivowels, consonants. You can learn more about their use in chapters 6 and 7 and about diphthongs in chapter 8.

Vowels:

1.	[i]	Ee	we, meet, key, sea, receive
2.	[ɪ]	Short I	with, gym, lily, listen
3.	[e]	Pure Ay	chaotic, dictates
4.	[ɛ]	Open Eh	enter, merry, many, friend
5.	[æ]	Short A	at, stab, act, shadow, magic
6.	[a]	Bright Ah	aisle (substitute #5 or #7)
7.	[ɑ]	Dark Ah	far, dark, calm, palm (silent l)
8.	[ɒ]	Short O	god, long (substitute #7)
9.	[ɔ]	Open O	chord, author, awe, shawl
10.	[o]	Pure Oh	hotel, obey
11.	[ʊ]	Short U	bush, foot, wolf, look
12.	[u]	Oo	flute, queue, noon, do, you
13.	[ʌ]	Uh	sung, up, son, come
14.	[ə]	Schwa	(2nd syl. of:) even, sofa, little
15.	[ɜ]	Er	learn, her, bird, journey, myrrh

Semivowels:

16.	[j]	Yah	yam, union, eulogy, pew, due
17.	[w]	Wah	was, witch, waste, once

Consonants:

18.	[m]	Em	sum, ma'am, dimmer, hymn
19.	[n]	En	nun, liner
20.	[ŋ]	Ing	sang, king, hunger, English
21.	[l]	El	love, wilt, Sally
22.	[r]	Ahr	red, earring, hear
23.	[h]	Aitch	house, hunk, Minnehaha
24.	[hw]	Which	why, whether, whiz
25.	[f]	Eff	far, feel, philosophy
26.	[v]	Vee	very, overt, quiver
27.	[θ]	Theta	thick, thistle, cloth
28.	[ð]	Edh	these, other, within, lathe
29.	[s]	Ess	sat, psalm, lets, decent
30.	[z]	Zee	zoom, buzzard, was, zest
31.	[ʃ]	Shah	shoe, negotiate, sugar, cash
32.	[ʒ]	Zsa-Zsa	leisure, garage, casual
33.	[p]	Pee	pay, caper, sup
34.	[b]	Bee	boy, saber, rub
35.	[t]	Tee	tent, ptomaine, slat
36.	[d]	Dee	die, leader, bed
37.	[k]	Kay	coal, choir, technique, anchor
38.	[g]	Hard Gee	girl, bigger, bug
39.	[tʃ]	Cha-Cha	'cello, rich, catcher
40.	[dʒ]	Soft Gee	jet, jasmine, ajar, huge

C Foreign Language Song Texts

Singing lets you relive experiences of people from many lands, expressed in their songs. You can do this by singing good English translations and sensing the national flavor of the music; or if you have some background in a foreign language, you and your teacher may agree that you can sing in that language.

The information given here does not provide a complete course in foreign language diction. That is not an appropriate goal for the first year of voice study. Your first priority now is to improve your singing, as to sound and technique. Your second priority, if you are not already a skilled musician, is to learn about music. If you have a desire to go beyond those two goals, you may enjoy exercising your new skills in a foreign language. If the foreign language causes a problem and distracts you from singing better, sing a translation or a different song.

You know that your first responsibility is to understand the poem completely, and that is true for foreign song texts. Many songs have singable English translations, but the meaning of the English version is naturally a little different from the original because of the need for rhythm and rhyme. This book gives literal translations at the foot of the music pages, using normal English word order. The following pages give translations of a third kind, made word-by-word so that you can see exactly what each word means.

Your next responsibility is to learn to pronounce the words correctly, and in these pages you will find IPA transcriptions to help you and a few general comments about how to sing in each language. Again, I want to stress that these comments do not tell all about every language—that would take many more pages. The intent is to give you the most essential information, so that if you have some background in the language and assistance from your teacher, you can do your song correctly and confidently.

What they all have in common

Besides English, the languages represented in this book are Italian (5 songs), German (5), Spanish (2), French (2), and Hebrew (1). They differ in the number of vowels used, but all of them have pure vowels, that is, no vowels that have diphthong shadings such as English has in "so" and "say." Also, in all of these languages the vowels always or most often have their Latin values, the ones used in the IPA. As examples, make it a habit to say [a] when you see the letter *a* and [i] when you see the letter *i*. Whatever vowel you sing, keep the quality of it pure for as long as the vowel lasts. Except for French, all of these languages have stronger (stressed) and weaker (unstressed) syllables. Transcriptions in this book indicate stress by underlining, but only when the musical rhythm creates some doubt or when there are two vowels in one syllable and one of them needs to be emphasized.

Songs in Italian

The art of singing as we know it comes from Italy, and many teachers prefer to have students sing in Italian before any other language. Italian is a legato language; the final sound of a word is nearly always connected smoothly to the first sound of the following word, forming an unbroken chain of sound until the time comes for you to breathe.

Italian vowels, not consonants, convey the energy and emotion of the language; the consonants are mostly soft, barely audible. Every stressed vowel followed by a single consonant is long, for example, *cane* [ka:ne].

Italian spelling often resembles IPA symbols, but there are some pitfalls. The letters *e* and *o* each have two pronunciations, closed and open, in stressed syllables, and the spelling does not indicate which one to use. Every *e* or *o* in a stressed syllable must be checked with a dictionary. (In unstressed syllables they are always closed.)

Consonants are gentle in Italian. [p, t, k] have no aspiration (explosiveness). [d, n, t, l] are all pronounced with the tongue lightly touching the upper teeth (dentalized). Further spelling pitfalls include *s* and *z*, which can be voiced or unvoiced, for example, *cosi* [kosi], not [kozi]. One must use a dictionary.

Italian double consonants are audibly different from single ones. If possible, the consonant sound continues for at least three times as long as it takes to say a single consonant, shown in IPA this way [m:m, s:s, b:b]. When the doubled consonant is a voiceless stop, there is silence between the closing and reopening of the consonant, for example, *attacca* [at:tak:ka]. This is an exception to the legato rule.

A new consonant sound, which is always pronounced as if doubled: [ʎ : ʎ] resembles [l:lj] but is made with the tip of the tongue down, not touching the palate.

New IPA symbols for Italian:

[:]	Lengthener	means "hold the position of the previous vowel or consonant."
[ʎ : ʎ]	Ell-Yah	svegliate [zveʎ:ʎate]
[ɾ]	Flipped R	caro [kaɾo], morire [moɾiɾe]

"Separazione," Giovanni Sgambati, page 116.

> [sepaɾatsio:ne dzovan:ni zgamba:ti]
> (Separation)
>
> doloro:sa spartɛntsa, ai   kwanto   ɛ du:ra
> Dolorosa spartenza, ahi, quanto   è duɾa!
> Sad   parting,   alas, how-much is hard,
>
> kwanto   ɛ grande per me la   pe:na ama:ɾa
> Quanto   è grande per me la   pena amara!
> How-much is great   for me the pain bitter!

"Lasciatemi morire," Claudio Monteverdi, page 130.
> [klaudjo monteveɾdi]
>
> laʃa:temi   moɾi:ɾe
> Lasciatemi morire!
> Let-me   die!
>
> e   ke   vole:te voi ke   mi konforte
> E   che   volete voi che mi conforte
> And what wish   you that me can-console

in kosi duːɾa sorte
In così dura sorte,
in such hard fate,

in kosi gran martiːɾe
In così gran martire?
in such great suffering?

"Vado ben spesso," Giovanni Bononcini, page 134.
[dzovan̲ːni bonontʃiːni]

vaːdo bɛn   spesːso kandʒando lɔːko
Vado ben   spesso cangiando loco
I-go indeed often, changing   place,

ma non sɔ   m̲ai kandʒar deziːo
Ma non so   mai cangiar desio.
but not I-know-how ever to-change desire.

sɛmpre listesːso saɾa   il m̲io fɔːko
Sempre l'istesso sarà   il mio foco
Always the-same will-be the my fire

e   saɾɔ   sɛmpre ank̲iːo
E   sarò   sempre anch'io
and will-be always also-I.

"Nina," Giovanni Battista Pergolesi, page 142.
[dzovanːni batːtista pergoleːzi]

tre   dʒorni son ke niːna
Tre   giorni son che Nina
Three days   are that Nina

in lɛtːto se   ne   sta
In letto se   ne   sta.
in bed   herself there stays.

il   sonːno lasːsasːsina
Il   sonno l'assassina,
The sleep   her-murders;

zveʎːʎatela per pjeta
Svegliatela   per pietà.
waken-her   for pity.

e   tʃimbali timpani pifːferi
E   cimbali, timpani, pifferi!
And cymbals, drums,   oboes!

zveʎːʎaːte m̲ia ninetːta
Svegliate   mia Ninetta
awaken   my dear-Nina

atːʃɔ   non dɔrma   pju
Acciò   non dorma   piú.
so-that not she-sleep more.

"Nel cor più non mi sento," Giovanni Paisiello, page 146.
[dzovan̲ːni paizjɛ̲lːlo]

nel   kɔr pju non mi   sɛnto
Nel   cor più non mi   sento
In-the heart more not myself I-feel

brilːlaːr la   dʒoventuː
Brillar la   gioventù:
shine   the youth;

kadzo:n del   mịo tormento
Cagion del   mio tormento,
cause   of-the my torture,

amo:r, sɛi kolpa tu
Amor, sei colpa tu.
Love, are guilty you.

mi stut:siki   mi mastiki
Mi stuzzichi,   mi mastichi,
Me you-pick-at, me you-bite,

mi pundziki mi pit:siki
Mi pungichi, mi pizzichi;
me you-prick, me you-pinch—

ke   kɔ:saɛ   kwesta ọimɛ
Che cosa   è questa, oimè!
what thing is this,   alas!

pjeta pjeta pjeta
Pietà, pietà, pietà!
Pity, pity, pity!

amo:rɛun   tʃɛrto   ke
Amore   è un certo   che,
Love   is a certain-thing that,

ke   delir̯a:r mi fa
Che delirar mi fa.
that to-rave me makes.

   ti   sɛnto si ti   sɛnto
2. Ti   sento, si, ti   sento,
   You I-hear, yes, you I-hear,

bɛl   fjo:r di dʒoventụ:
Bel   fior   di gioventù: . . .
beautiful flower of youth, . . .

a:nima mịa sɛi tu
Anima mia, sei tu. . . .
soul   mine, are you. . . .

kwel vi:zoạun tʃɛrto   ke
Quel viso ha un certo   che . . .
That face has a certain-something that . . .

Songs in Spanish

Like Italian, Spanish is normally legato, and vowels carry the expressive message. Spanish [a] is a little less bright than in Italian, and [i o u] are all a little more open. In phonetic transcription [e] always stands for the vowel "e", but it is pronounced much more open than Italian [e]. The closed, bright [e] is heard only in the combinations "ei", "ey" and "ell". For instance, in "estrella" (star) the first "e" is open and the second is closed.

For the most part Spanish consonants are even softer than Italian consonants. "B" and "v" are spoken identically, a slight buzz with air passing between the lips; IPA uses [b] for both consonants. "D" and "t" are dentalized, but less far forward than in Italian. "D" between vowels (even if the vowels are in different words) is pronounced [ð], Edh. "J" is an exaggerated [h]. "R" is flipped [ɾ], and "rr" is heavily rolled [rr]. "Ll" in Spanish/Castilian texts is [ʎ], but in Latin American texts is [j]. "N" with a tilde, "ñ", sounds somewhat like [nj] but is produced with the tongue touching the lower teeth; the IPA symbol is [ɲ].

New IPA symbol for Spanish:

[ɲ]	Enya	señor [seɲor], cariño [kariɲo]

"El Tecolote," page 000.

tekolote e   gwaðjana
Tecolote de   Guadiana,
Owl   from Guadiana,

paharo madrugaðor
Pajaro madrugador;
bird   early-riser;

para ke bwelas de notʃe
Para que vuelas de noche,
Why (--) you-fly at night

ai tenjendo por sujo   el di̯a
Ay, teniendo por suyo   el dia,
Ah, having   for yourself the day?

pobresito tekolote
Pobrecito tecolote,
poor-little owl,

ja   se   kansa ðe bolar
Ya   se   cansa de volar.
already itself tires of flying.

"La Paloma," Sebastián Yradier, page 166.
[la paloma sebastji̯an iraðjeɾ]

kwando sali de   labana   balgame dos
Cuando salí de   la   Habana, válgame Dios!
When   I-left from the   Havana, bless-me God!

naðje mea   bisto salir si no fwi   yo
Nadie me ha   visto salir, si no fuí   yo,
nobody me has seen leave, if not it-was I.

una linda hwatʃinaŋga   aja   boj jo
Una linda Guachinanga,   alla voy yo,
a   pretty girl-from-Mexico-City, there go I,

se   vino ðetras de mi ke si seɲor
Se   vino detras de mí, que sí señor.
herself came after of me, (-) yes, sir!

sia tu   bentana jega   una paloma
Si a tu   ventana llega   una paloma,
If at your window arrives a   dove,

tratala kon kariɲo kes   mi persona
Trátala con cariño que es   mi persona,
treat-it with love   for it-is my person.

kwentala tus amoɾes   bjen de mi biða
Cuentala tus amores   bien de mi vida,
Tell-it   your love-feelings, good of my life,

koɾonala ðe floɾes kes   kosa mi̯a
Coronala de flores que   es cosa mia.
crown-it with flowers, because it-is thing mine.

ai tʃinita   ke si ai ke ðame   tu̯amor
Ay chinita   que sí! Ay que dame   tu   amor!
O little-one, but yes! O but give-me your love!

ai ke bente konmigo tʃinita   aðonde bibo jo
Ay que vente conmigo chinita,   adonde vivo yo!
O but come with-me little-one, to-where live I!

el di̱ ke nos   kasemos   balgame ðjos
2. El dia que nos   casemos, válgame Dios,
   The day that each-other we-marry, bless-me God!

en   laiglesja katedral   aja   boj jo
En la iglesia catedral,   alla voy yo,
in the church   cathedral, there go   I,

desde la   iglesiauntitos   ke si seɲor
Desde la   iglesia juntitos, que sí señor,
from   the church together,   (-) yes sir!

nos iɾemos a ðormir aja   boj jo
Nos iremos a dormir, alla voy yo. Si a tu ventana . . .
we will-go to sleep, there go I.

Songs in French

French pronunciation is not more difficult than that of other languages in this book, but the spelling is. French spelling is as difficult for French speakers as English spelling is for us.

In French all syllables are equal, that is, no syllables are stressed by being louder than those around them. Make your French syllables extremely even, but when you reach the end of a phrase or breath, slightly prolong the vowel of the last syllable (not counting a schwa). In order to emphasize the smooth connections of legato French, Dr. Pierre Delattre recommended transcribing each syllable as a separate unit; it is hard to guess the French spelling by seeing the IPA version.

Nasalized vowels are characteristic of French; to make them, the soft palate drops, allowing more breath to flow through the nose than through the mouth. Normally, French speakers produce the non-nasalized vowels with the soft palate lifted to prevent any air from going through the nose.

Mixed vowels (not diphthongs) are also characteristic; to make them, the lips round, but the tongue rises forward. (In English, when the lips round, the tongue pulls back automatically.) We will call these three vowels by their components: [y], called Ee-Oo, is made by raising the tongue as if for [i] and *simultaneously* rounding the lips for [u]. For [ø], called Ay-Oh, the tongue rises as if for [e] and the lips round for [o]. For [œ], called Open E-O, the tongue rises as if for [ɛ] and the lips round for [ɔ].

Besides [j] and [w], French has one more semivowel, [ɥ], made by starting from [y] and gliding to the following vowel sound. In the word "nuit" [nɥi], the tongue remains lifted, but the lips lose their rounding, changing the vowel sound from [y] to [i].

If you have studied spoken French, you will notice two main differences in sung French: "mute e" is pronounced as [ə]; and the "French," uvular [ʀ] is replaced with a flipped or rolled [r].

New IPA symbols for French:

[ã]	Nasalized Ah	an [ã], enfant [ãfã]
[ɛ̃]	Nasalized Eh	hein [ɛ̃], point [pwɛ̃]
[ɔ̃]	Nasalized Oh	on [ɔ̃], sont [sɔ̃]
[œ̃]	Nasalized Open E-O	un [œ̃]
[y]	Ee-Oo	du [dy]
[ø]	Ay-Oh	feu [fø]
[œ]	Open E-O	fleur [flœr], leur [lœr]
[ɥ]	Ee-Oo Glide	nuit [nɥi]

Auprès de ma blonde, page 102.

      o   ʒa rdɛ̃ də mɔ̃ pɛ rə
1. Au   jardin de mon père
     At-the garden of my   father

lɛ lo rje   sɔ̃   flœ ri
Les lauriers sont fleuri,
the laurels are   flowered;

tu   lɛ   zwa zo dy   mɔ̃ də
Tous les oiseaux du   monde
all   the birds   of-the world

vɔ̃   ti   fɛ rə   lœ   rni
Vont y   faire leur nids . . .
go   and make their nests . . .

     la   kaj   la   tu rtə rɛ lə
2. La   caill', la tourterelle
    The quail, the turtledove,

e   lə   ʒɔli   pɛ rdri
Et le joli   perdrix,
and the pretty partridge

e   la blɑ̃ ʃə   kɔlɔ̃ bə
Et   la blanche colombe,
and the white   dove,

ki   ʃɑ̃ tə   ʒu re nɥi
Qui chante jour et   nuit
who sings day and night . . .

    ɛl   ʃɑ̃ tə   pu   rlɛ fi jə
3. Ell' chante pour les filles
   She sings   for   the girls

ki   nɔ̃   pwɛ̃ də ma ri
Qui n'ont   point de mari;
who not-have any   of husband;

sɛ   pɑ pu   rmwa kɛl   ʃɑ̃ tə
C'est pas pour moi qu'ell' chante,
it-is not for me   that-she sings,

kar   ʒɑ   ne œ̃ ʒɔ li
Car   j'en   ai un joli.
because I-of-them have a   pretty (one).

       oprɛ   də ma blɔ̃ də
Refrain: Auprès de ma blonde
       Close   to my blonde (wife)

kil   fɛ   bɔ̃   dɔr mir
Qu'il fait bon dormir!
how-it does good to-sleep!

"Hébé," Ernest Chausson, page 170.
[e be ɛr nɛst ʃo sɔ̃]

lɛ zjø bɛ se   ru ʒi sɑ̃   te   kɑ̃ di də
Les yeux baissés, rougissante et   candide,
The eyes lowered, blushing   and innocent,

vɛ   rlœ rbɑ̃ kɛ kɑ̃   e be sa vɑ̃ sɛ
Vers leur banquet quand Hébé s'avançait,
toward their feast   when Hebe herself-drew-near,

lɛ djø ʃa rme tɑ̃ dɛ   lœ rku pə vi də
Les dieux charmés tendaient leur coupe vide,
the gods, charmed, held-out their cup   empty

e   də   nɛ ktar lɑ̃ fɑ̃   la rɑ̃ pli sɛ
Et   de   nectar l'enfant   la remplissait.
and with nectar the-child it re-filled.

nu   tus o si   kɑ̃   pa sə la ʒœ nɛ sə
Nous tous aussi, quand passe la jeunesse,
We   all   also, when passes the youth,

nu   lɥi   tɑ̃ dɔ̃   nɔ trə ku   pa lɑ̃ vi
Nous lui   tendons notre coupe à l'envi.
we   to-it hold-out our   cup in the-emulation.

kɛ   lɛ lə vɛ̃   ki   vɛ rsə la de ɛsə
Quel est le vin qu'y   verse la déesse?
What is the wine that-there pours the goddess?

nu   li ɲɔ rɔ̃   i lɑ̃ ni   vre ra vi
Nous l'ignorons; il enivre   et ravit.
We   it-know-not; it intoxicates and delights.

a jɑ̃   su ri   dɑ̃ sa grɑ si mmɔ rtɛ lə
Ayant souri dans sa grâce immortelle,
Having smiled in   her grace immortal,

e be se lwa ɲə   ɔ̃   la ra pɛ   lɑ̃ vɛ̃
Hébé s'éloigne; on la rappelle en vain.
Hebe goes away; one her calls-back in vain.

lɔ̃ tɑ̃   zɑ̃ kɔr sy rla ru   te tɛ rnɛ lə
Longtemps encor sur la   route éternelle,
Long   yet   on the road eternal,

nɔ   trœ jɑ̃ plœ r sɥi   le ʃɑ̃ sɔ̃   di vɛ̃
Notre oeil en pleurs suit l'échanson   divin.
our   eye in tears   follows the-cup-bearer divine.

Songs in German

German and English come from the same roots and are both classed as Germanic languages. Characteristics of Germanic languages include: strong syllabic stress; energetic consonants; non-legato articulation; aspiration (breathiness) of sounds such as [h], [p], [t], and [k].

A significant feature of German is vowel length: compare "satt" [zat], which has a short vowel, with "Saal" [sa:l], which has a long one. Precise time-studies of speech have shown that even in rapid conversation a native German takes more time to say a long vowel than a short one. If a short vowel occurs in singing a note, it is sung as short as possible and the following consonant takes up part of the rhythmic value. A long vowel, by contrast, is stretched to fill as much of the note value as possible.

German uses the three mixed vowels described for French, plus one more: [ʏ], Short I-U, with the tongue lifted for [ɪ] and the lips rounded for [ʊ].

Also typical of German are the two sounds of "ch." Form your mouth to say [ɪ], then make a soft noise by blowing air through the opening; the resulting sound is [ç], which Germans call the "Ich sound." Next form your mouth to say [a], then make a soft noise by blowing through the opening; the sound is [x], called the "Ach sound." The difference between "Ich" and "Ach" occurs automatically as a result of the preceding sound; there is little chance of saying the wrong one. Most Americans overdo these sounds; keep them light and soft.

The German "r" has varied forms, somewhat subject to personal taste. Avoid the American [r]; use flipped [ɾ] and tongue-rolled [r], more or less as in Italian.

IPA symbols needed for German:

[y]	Ee-Oo	Güte [gy:tə], über [y:bər]
[ʏ]	Short I-U	entrückt [ɛntrʏkt]
[ø]	Ay-O	krönst [krø̜nst],
[œ]	Open E-O	Schöpfer [ʃœ pfər]
[ç]	Ich sound	reicht [raeçt], ewig [e:vɪç]
[x]	Ach sound	Hauch [haox], Baches [baxəs]

"Bald wehen uns des Frühlings Lüfte," Franz Joseph Haydn, page 151.

[frants j̲o̲zɛf h̲aedən]

balt ve:ən ᴜns dɛs   fry:lɪŋs   lʏftə
Bald wehen uns des   Frühlings Lüfte
Soon blow   to-us of-the spring   breezes,

balt vɪrt   der dᴜŋklə h̲aen bəle:pt
Bald wird   der dunkle Hain belebt,
soon will-become the dark   grove enlivened;

ɛs   latmən ʃo:n der   kro̲ətər dʏftə
Es   atmen   schon der   Kräuter Düfte,
there breathe already of—the herbs   scents,

ɪndɛs zɪç je:dər za:mən re:kt
ɪndes sich jeder Samen regt.
while itself every seed   rouses.

a̲ox lᴜns ʃt̲aekt vɔn:nə h̲o̲ət hɛrni:dər
Auch uns   steigt Wonne heut hernieder,
Also to-us climbs joy   today downward,

da   vi:r d̲aen na:mənsfɛst bəge:n
Da   wir dein Namensfest begehn;
because we your name-day   celebrate;

fɛrnɪm   o: mɛnʃənfro̲ønt   di: li:dər
Vernimm, o Menschenfreund, die Lieder,
hear,   o humanitarian,   the songs;

der ʃœpfər hø:rə   ᴜnzər fle:n
Der Schöpfer höre   unser Fleh'n.
the Creator   may-hear our   pleading.

"Bitten," Ludwig van Beethoven, page 153.

[bɪt̲:tən l̲u:tvɪç fan b̲e̲:tho:fən]

gɔt d̲aenə gy:tə   r̲aeçt zo: v̲aet
Gott, deine Güte   reicht so weit,
God, your goodness reaches as far

zo v̲aet   di: v̲ɔlkən ge:ən
So weit   die Wolken gehen,
as far [as] the clouds go.

du: krø:nst ᴜns mɪt   barmh̲ɛrtsɪçkaet
Du krönst uns mit   Barmherzigkeit,
You crown us   with compassion

ᴜnt a̲elst ᴜns b̲aetsuʃte:ən
Und eilst, uns beizustehen.
and hurry us   by-to-stand.

hɛr   m̲aenə bᴜrk   m̲aen fɛls   m̲aen hɔrt
Herr, meine Burg,   mein Fels, mein Hort,
Lord, my   fortress, my   rock, my   protection,

fɛrnɪm   maen fleːn,   mɛrk |aof maen vɔrt
Vernimm mein Flehn,   merk' auf mein Wort,
Hear   my   pleading, notice   my   word,

dɛn   ɪc   vɪl   foːr   diːr   beːtən
Denn ich will   vor   dir   beten!
for   I   want before you to-pray.

"An die Musik," Franz Schubert, page 156.
[an di: muziːk, frants ʃuːbərt]

duː hɔldə kʊnst ɪn viːfiːl   graoən ʃtʊnden
Du holde Kunst, in wieviel   grauen Stunden,
You lovely art,   in how-many gray   hours,

voː   mɪç dɛs leːbəns vɪldər kraes |ʊmʃtrɪkt
Wo   mich des Lebens wilder Kreis umstrickt,
where me   the life's   wild   ring around-binds,

hast duː maen hɛrts tsu: varmər liːp |ɛntːtsʊndən
Hast du   mein Herz zu warmer Lieb' entzunden,
have you my   heart to warm   love kindled,

hast   mɪç ɪn   aenə bɛsrə vɛlt |ɛntrʏkt
Hast   mich in   eine bessre Welt entrückt!
have-you me   into a   better world wafted-away!

ɔft   hat |aen zɔøftsər daenər   harf |ɛntflɔsən
Oft   hat ein Seufzer, deiner   Harf' entflossen,
often has a   sigh,   from-your harp flowed-away,

aen zyːsər haelɪgər akːkɔrt fɔn diːr
Ein süsser, heiliger Akkord von dir,
a   sweet, holy   chord   from you,

dɛn hɪmːməl bɛsrər   tsaetən miːr |ɛrʃlɔsən
Den Himmel bessrer   Zeiten mir   erschlossen,
the heaven of-better times   to-me opened;

duː hɔldə kʊnst |ɪç daŋkə diːr dafyːr
Du holde Kunst, ich danke dir dafür!
you lovely art,   I   thank you for-that.

"Wanderers Nachtlied," Franz Schubert, page 158.
[vandərərs naxtliːt frants ʃuːbərt

yːbər alːlən gɪpfəln
Über allen   Gipfeln
Over all   mountain-peaks

ɪst ruː
Ist Ruh,
is rest,

in alːlən vɪpfəln
In allen   Wipfeln
in all   tree-tops

ʃpyːrəst duː
Spürest du
feel   you

kaom aenən haox
Kaum einen Hauch;
hardly a   breath;

diː føːklaen ʃvaegən   ɪm   valdə
Die Vöglein schweigen im   Walde
the little-birds are-silent in-the forest.

vartə nu:r baldə
Warte nur, balde
Wait   only, soon

ru:əst du: ḷaox
Ruhest du   auch.
rest   you also.

"Widmung," Robert Franz, page 162.
[vɪtmuŋ   ro:bert frants]

o: daŋkə nɪçt fy:r di:zə li:dər
O danke nicht für diese Lieder,
O thank not   for these songs,

mi:r tsi:mt ɛs daŋkbar di:r   tsu: zaen
Mir   ziemt es dankbar dir   zu sein;
to-me suits it thankful to-you to   be.

du: ga:pst zi: mi:r ɪç ge:bə vi:dər
Du gabst sie   mir, ich gebe wieder
You gave them to-me; I   give back

vas jetst ʊnt aenst ʊnt e:vɪç   daen
Was jetzt und einst und ewig   dein.
what now and soon and eternally yours.

daen zɪnt zi: al:lə ja   gəve:zən
Dein sind sie alle ja   gewesen;
Yours have they all   indeed been;

aos   daenər li:bən aogən lɪçt
Aus deiner lieben Augen Licht
from your   dear   eyes' light

hap ɪç zi: trɔølɪç apgəle:zən
Hab ich sie   treulich abgelesen:
have I   them truly   read-off:

kɛnst du: di: aegnən li:dər nɪçt
Kennst du   die eignen Lieder nicht?
know you the own   songs not?

"Ach Lieb, ich muss nun scheiden," Richard Strauss, page 174.
                            [rɪçart ʃtraos]

ax   li:p ɪç mʊs nu:n ʃaedən
Ach Lieb, ich muss nun scheiden,
Ah love, I   must now leave,

ge:n y:bər bɛrk   ʊnt ta:l
Gehn über Berg   und Tal,
go   over mountain and valley.

di: ɛrlən ʊnt di: vaedən
Die Erlen und die Weiden,
The alders and the willows,

di: vaenən altsuma:l
Die weinen allzumal.
they weep   together.

zi: za:n zo: ɔft ʊns vandərn
Sie   sahn so oft   uns wandern
They saw so often us   walk

tsuzam:mən an baxəs   rant
Zusammen an Baches Rand,
together   on brook's edge.

das laenə loːn   den landərn
Das Eine ohn'   den Andern
The one   without the other

geːt yːbər iːrən fɛrʃtant
Geht über ihren Verstand.
goes over their understanding.

diː ɛrlən ʊnt diː vaedən
Die Erlen und die Weiden
The alders and the willows

foːr ʃmɛrts ɪn trɛːnən ʃteːn
Vor Schmerz in Tränen stehn,
for pain   in tears   are;

nuːn dɛŋkət   viː ʊns baedən
Nun denket,   wie uns beiden
now think-you how we two

eːrst mʊs tsuː hɛrtsən geːn
Erst muss zu Herzen gehn.
just must to heart   go.

A song in Hebrew

The "ch" sound is pronounced [x] as in German "Bach."
"Hinay ma tov," Israeli folk song, p. 98.

IPA: [hi neI ma   tov uma   naim
     Hinay ma   tov uma   naim
     Behold what-is good and-what-is pleasant:

ʃɛ vɛt   axim   gam jaxad
shevet   achim   gam yachad.
to-remain brothers also together.

D Glossary of Vocal and Musical Terms

A tempo in a steady tempo, used especially after an interruption or temporary change of tempo.

Adagio at a tempo slower than andante.

Adam's apple a protuberance in front of the neck formed by the Thyroid cartilage.

Agility ability to sing a series of quick notes rapidly.

Al fine to the end, i.e., repeat until the word *fine*.

Alla coda to the coda, i.e., skip to the conclusion.

Allegretto in a somewhat lively tempo, less quick than allegro.

Allegro in a lively tempo.

Alto a low female voice, especially in choral music.

Andante in a slow tempo, at a walking pace.

Andantino in a moderately slow tempo, quicker than andante.

Appoggiatura an ornamental melodic tone, often written small.

Aria air; an Italian vocal composition; an elaborate solo in an opera, cantata, or oratorio.

Arpeggio notes of a chord sung or played in succession.

Articulation aspect of diction, relating to consonant clarity.

Art song an accompanied vocal composition with artistic intent.

Arytenoid cartilages two small ladle-shaped cartilages whose movement adjusts the position of the posterior end of the vocal bands.

Aspirate (verb) to expel with a sound of moving air; (adj.) characterized by a sound of moving air.

Attack (noun or verb) beginning of a tone.

Balanced tone singing production with complete coordination between the action of the vocal cords and the action of the variable resonators.

Ballad a narrative folk song that uses the same melody for each stanza; a gentle, expressive pop song.

Baritone a male voice of medium range, between tenor and bass.

Baroque a musical style that was current roughly from 1600–1750; composers include Monteverdi, Purcell, Bach, and Handel.

Bass the lowest male voice type; the lowest note of a chord; a low-pitched stringed instrument.

Belt (verb, slang) deliver forcefully.

Belt voice a technique of energized singing with high laryngeal position and little sensation of escaping air (source: Jo Estill, NATS master class, 1985).

Blended register a series of notes of medium pitch that have some qualities of light registration and some of heavy registration.

Breath control, breath management the art and skill of supplying the right amount of air at the right degree of pressure to perform music artistically.

Breathy tone an inefficient vocal tone accompanied by the sound of escaping air, caused by incomplete closure of the vocal bands during tone production.

Bridge the point at which the singer is aware of passing from one vocal register to another.

Cantabile in a lyric, legato singing style.

Cantata a vocal composition for solo and/or chorus, usually in several sections called movements.

Catch breath a quick, partial refilling of the lungs.

Change of voice the lowering of a teenager's voice during puberty, caused by the growth of the larynx and the vocal bands.

Chest thorax, the section of the body enclosed by the ribs, breastbone, upper spine, and diaphragm.

Chest register chest voice, heavy register, notes of the lower range made with thick vocal cords; the usual speech range of men and the majority of women. (So-called because of detectable sympathetic vibrations in the rib cage.)

Chord two or more notes sounded simultaneously.

Chorus choir; refrain or recurring portion of a song.

Classical a musical style that was current from roughly 1750–1825; composers include Haydn, Mozart, and early Beethoven.

Clavicular breathing breathing by raising and lowering the chest, as exhausted athletes do when they need to exchange large quantities of air without concern for control (named after the collarbone or clavicle).

Coda literally, tail; concluding section.

Con anima with soul, with spirit.

Consonants speech sounds produced with partial or complete stoppage of breath flow.

Continuants consonant sounds capable of being prolonged.

Contralto a formal term for a low female voice used in opera or concert music.

Crescendo getting louder, abbr. cresc.

Cricoid cartilage a ring-shaped cartilage at the top of the windpipe, the basis of the larynx.

Crooning a casual style of singing pop songs with a microphone.

Da capo literally, from the head, i.e., return to the beginning, abbr. D. C.

Dal segno from the sign, i.e., return to the given sign, abbr. D. S.

Descrescendo diminuendo, getting softer, abbr. decresc.

Delicato delicately.

Diaphragm a large dome-shaped muscular membrane that separates the chest from the abdominal cavity, active in inhalation.

Diaphragmatic-costal breathing a method of breath management that employs expansion and muscular action in the lower ribs, waist area, and abdomen externally and the diaphragm internally.

Diction formation and delivery of the words of vocal music.

Diphthong combination of two vowel sounds in one syllable.

Duet a musical composition for two performers.

Dynamics degrees of loudness and softness.

Enunciation an aspect of diction concerned with production and clarity of vowels and syllables.

Epigastrium the upper area of the abdomen, above the waist and below the ribs.

Epiglottis leaf-shaped cartilage that lowers to cover the larynx during swallowing.

Exhalation expiration, breathing out.

Expression the act of making feelings and thoughts known to others.

Falsetto a light, high register of the male voice made with thin vocal bands.

False vocal bands false vocal cords, two projecting muscular flaps lying just above the "true" vocal bands.

Flexibility ability of the voice to sing with agility and to produce sudden changes in pitch, dynamics, and quality.

Focus a sense of concentrated vibratory energy.

Folk song a song that is widely known, transmitted chiefly from person-to-person without being written down, even though the original composer of the song may be known. A folk song is normally performed with an improvised accompaniment (one not precisely written out in musical notation) or with no accompaniment, except for artistic arrangements made by someone other than the composer. This describes the songs in the "Traditional Songs" portion of this book.

Forcing singing with effort, when unnecessary muscular action interferes with the desired actions of singing.

Free tone an unrestrained, spontaneously produced sound without any evidence of rigid tension.

Frequency rate of vibrations (cycles) per second, expressed in Hertz, e.g., A above middle C = 440 Hz.

Fundamental the basic tone produced by the whole of a vibrating mass, having a lower frequency than any of the overtones.

Glottal attack onset of a tone produced by blowing the closed vocal bands apart with a sharp, coughlike sound.

Glottis the opening between the vocal bands.

Hard palate bony front portion of the roof of the mouth.

Harmony the art of arranging chords artistically.

Head register head voice, light register, higher tones of the voice, made with thin vocal bands (so-called because of perceived sympathetic vibrations in the head.)

Hertz cycles per second, abbr. Hz.

Hum produce pitches while exhaling through the nose.

Hyoid bone U-shaped bone that anchors the base of the tongue.

Inflection pitch variation of the speaking voice.

Inhalation inspiration, breathing in.

Intercostal muscles short muscles between the ribs, active in inhalation.

Interpretation the art of re-creating the music imagined by a composer on the basis of written musical notation.

Intonation degree of accuracy in producing pitches.

Involuntary not resulting from conscious intention.

Key the organization of tones in relation to a keynote, tonic note, or tonal center. The concept of key includes a perceived need for a piece of music to reach a final point of rest on the keynote.

Laryngoscope an instrument invented by Manuel Garcia, 1855, for examining the larynx, consisting of a dental mirror and a focused light source.

Larynx voice box, cartilaginous enclosure that surrounds the vocal bands.

Legato connected, with no discernable break in sound.

Leggiero e distintamente lightly and distinctly.

Lied German art song (plural, lieder).

Lyric text of a pop song.

Major scale a scale with a major 3rd between the first and third notes. (See chapter 12.)

Melody tones in succession, perceived as a musical line.

Minor scale a scale with a minor 3rd between the first and third notes. (See chapter 12.)

Meter the division of music into measures or bars, each with a specific number of beats.

Mezzo-soprano female voice of medium range, especially in opera and concert music.

Moderato in a medium tempo.

Molto very much.

Musical short for "musical play," a play with a significant number of songs.

Nasality a distortion of tone caused by too much air passing above a lowered soft palate and through the nose.

Node nodule, a swelling on the edge of one vocal band, caused by the natural healing process that follows overuse or irritation of the vocal bands.

Octave distance between a note and the nearest note with the same name.

Opera a theatrical entertainment with (nearly) all of the text sung rather than spoken.

Oratorio a lengthy religious work for soloists and chorus meant for concert performance, i.e. not staged.

Overtone a tone produced by vibration of a fraction of a vibrating body, thus a higher tone than the fundamental.

Pharynx throat, the cavity behind the mouth, between the larynx and the nose.

Phonetics the science of speech sounds and their representation through written symbols.

Phrase (vocal) a series of notes sung on one breath; (musical) a series of melodic notes perceived as an expressive unit analogous to a clause or sentence in verbal language. (A musical phrase is not limited by breath capacity and may embrace several vocal phrases.)

Phrasing the art of shaping music expressively, including decisions as to when to breathe.

Pitch a property of tone, resulting from frequency of vibration, e.g., high pitch, low pitch.

Poco mosso a little (more) motion, quicker.

Projection transmitting the text and tone from the singer to the most distant members of an audience.

Pronunciation aspect of diction, including correctness of speech sounds.

Pure vowel a single vowel sound without diphthong coloring.

Range distance between the highest and lowest note of a song or of a person's voice.

Refrain a recurring chorus or phrase that follows different stanzas of a song.

Register a series of similar-sounding notes produced by a similar mechanism or vocal adjustment (named after a row of similar pipes on a pipe organ).

Release end of a tone.

Repertoire the list of pieces that a musician is ready to perform on short notice.

Resonance intensification of a musical sound by sympathetic vibration.

Resonators cavities whose size and shape cause air in them to vibrate sympathetically with a sound source, e.g., the vocal bands, strengthening and reinforcing the sound.

Rhythm patterns created by the relative length, loudness, and perceived importance of notes.

Ritardando slowing down, abbr. rit.

Ritenuto held back, abbr. rit.

Romantic a musical style prevalent in the 1800s; composers include Beethoven (in his later compositions), Schumann, Verdi, Wagner.

Scale a series of pitches arranged in order of frequency within an octave, most commonly seven-toned scales called major and minor.

Soft palate velum, soft portion of the roof of the mouth.

Soprano highest female voice; highest part in a choir.

Sostenuto in a sustained, legato manner.

Staccato detached, not connected.

Straight tone a tone that lacks vibrato.

Strophic constructed in stanzas, each sung to the same melody.

Tempo rate of speed in music.

Tenor highest male voice.

Tenuto held, slightly lengthened, abbr. ten.

Thorax see Chest.

Throat see Pharynx.

Through composed not composed in repetitive stanzas.

Thyro-arytenoid muscles the muscular body of the vocal bands.

Thyroid cartilage the largest cartilage of the larynx, forming its sides.

Timbre tone quality, the distinctive character of a tone, caused by the cumulative effect of the fundamental and its overtones.

Tone a musical sound of a definite pitch and timbre.

Trachea windpipe.

Tremolo a vibrato that is faulty in being too wide, too fast, or too slow; (instrumental) rapid repetition of a tone.

Trill regular, rapid alternation of a tone and its neighbor.

Triphthong a combination of three vowels in one syllable.

Unvoiced consonants made without vocal band vibration.

Uvula the small mass of flesh that hangs down from the soft palate above the tongue.

Vamp repeat an accompaniment pattern until the singer is ready to begin singing.

Velum soft palate.

Vibrato regular oscillation of a tone above and below a perceived pitch center, also slightly affecting the timbre and loudness of the tone.

Vocal bands vocal cords, two muscular folds formed by the thyro-arytenoid muscles, capable of closing over the windpipe and of vibrating in response to air pressure from the lungs, resulting in vocal tone.

Vocal tract the various organs from the lungs to the lips that collaborate to produce speech and singing.

Voice box larynx.

Voiced consonants made with vocal band vibration.

Volume perceived loudness of tone.

Vowel speech unit (phoneme) characterized by unimpeded flow of breath.

Whisper breathy speech made without vocal band vibration (although the bands are held in contact with each other along part of their length).

Index of Persons
and Song Sources

Index of Vocal and Musical Terms

Use this page to jot down more exercises or to begin composing your own songs!

Use this page to jot down more exercises or to begin composing your own songs!